When You're the One Who Cheats:

Ten Things You Need to Know

Dr. Tammy Nelson

In her no holds barred, honest look at cheating in the 21st century, Dr. Tammy Nelson offers a helpful road map for those who want to create lives filled with passion, joy and integrity.

— **Michele Weiner-Davis**, Author of *Healing from Infidelity*

Dr. Tammy Nelson is a pioneer in the field of relationships, sexuality, and affairs. "When You're the One Who Cheats" is an important, insightful, and non-judgmental book for individuals and couples.

— **Barry McCarthy**, Best-selling author of *Rekindling Desire*

The book is relentlessly honest...anyone looking for understanding, humanity, and utter lack of judgment will find much of value in this guide.

— **Stephen Snyder MD**. Author, *Love Worth Making*

**When You're The One Who Cheats:
Ten Things You Need To Know**

ISBN: 978-1-9994810-0-1 (paperback)

ISBN: 978-1-9994810-1-8 (pdf e-book)

Table of Contents

CHAPTER THREE
Tell or Don't, But Don't Blame Your Spouse

CHAPTER FOUR
Stop Saying You're Sorry

CHAPTER FIVE
Sometimes It's Just Chemistry

CHAPTER SIX
Sometimes It's a Mistake

CHAPTER SEVEN
Sometimes You Fall in Love

CHAPTER EIGHT

Should I Stay or Should I Go?

CHAPTER NINE:

Creating A New Vision

CHAPTER TEN

Can You Have It All?

ACKNOWLEDGEMENTS

I would like to acknowledge all the people who helped with the birth of this book. If I leave some of you out, I am truly sorry for that. Please know I am so grateful to all of you.

First, let me thank Isabella Mise and Paul Keable for giving me the idea to write another book, and for agreeing that there needed to be another viewpoint on infidelity, one that had never been done before, and for giving me access to the amazing statistics in this book. Thank you to Ryan Lannon for his quick responses to all of my questions all of the time and to Peter Kyriazis for his design talents.

Thank you Nicole de Montbrun and Lynda Spark for your editorial direction and I am so sorry for both of your losses during the time you worked on this book. Thank for your open minds and commitment to this project and its quick turnaround.

Thank you to everyone who talked with me about their personal experiences, all of the cheaters, those who found solace in an outside relationship, the ones who regretted it and the ones who made it work and are still with both an inside and an outside partner. Your honesty and courage helped me gain perspective and understand the truth of infidelity.

With deep appreciation and respect for all of the couples and individuals who have been in my office and in my workshops who have struggled with infidelity and its aftermath, and who trust me with their most private pain, hopes and dreams. Please know that none of you are in this book yet all are represented on some level, as we are all human.

And thank you to all of the therapists who have been in my trainings and come to me for supervision with their cases. Yes, this is the hardest work you will ever do, and the most rewarding. Thank you for sharing with me. I have loved walking this path beside you.

Thank you to Alicia Walker, Wednesday Martin, Janis Abrahms Spring, Katherine Woodward Thomas, Michele Weiner-Davis, Stephen Snyder, Esther Perel, and all of the other experts quoted who have kindly contributed their brilliance.

Thanks to my amazing children, Tyler and Emma, and to Lauren and Nicole, for loving me and letting me love them.

I want to acknowledge all of the amazing friendships in my life, particularly Doug and Andy; here's to lifelong support and spiritual monogamy.

And to my forever husband, Bruce Hirshfield for his belief in me, now and always.

DEDICATION:

To my friend and mentor Dr. Gina Ogden
– who reminded us all that women love sex.
You will be missed.

Any similarity to real or imagined persons
in this book is coincidence. All names have
been changed to protect the guilty.

"The best lack all conviction,
while the worst are full of
passionate intensity"

- William Butler Yeats

TEN THINGS EVERY CHEATER SHOULD KNOW

ONE: You're the One Who Cheated

TWO: It Doesn't Matter Why You Did It

THREE: Tell or Don't; but Don't Blame Your Spouse

FOUR: Stop Saying I'm Sorry

FIVE: Sometimes It's Just Chemistry

SIX: Sometimes It's a Mistake

SEVEN: Sometimes You Fall in Love

EIGHT: You Can Stay or Go

NINE: Create a New Vision

TEN: You Can't Have it All

Introduction

When You're the One Who Cheats: Ten Things You Need to Know is a book for anyone having an affair or indiscretion of any kind and who is confused, unsure and looking for answers. When you're the one who cheats it can feel like you have no options. This book can help.

This is a book for men and women (straight, LGBTQIA and unisexual) who identify as cheaters. It's also for anyone who's been thinking of having an affair. It offers a clear, direct and expert look at what you might be facing once you choose to go down the path of cheating on your spouse or committed partner. Reading this can also help you decide if you should end your affair or your marriage, and it will help once you are in recovery from either or both. No matter how you use this book, if you read it and do the simple exercises provided, you'll find answers. And you will realize that, yes, you do have options.

Throughout, I provide nonjudgmental explanations, advice and a non-pathological view of infidelity, in all its permutations, to help you—the cheating partner—evaluate your situation and make some choices. My aim is to help you, the cheating partner, find clarity.

There's advice to help you figure out why you cheated, and decide if you should tell your spouse about the affair, and advice on how to have that difficult conversation. There are also practical exercises and questionnaires designed to help you decide important matters such as "Should I Stay or Should I Go?" with dialogues and checklists to help you determine how to "End Your Affair with Integrity," if that's what you want, and a section on how to decide if, instead, your outside partner is really the one for you.   There are clearly laid-out worksheets and steps to follow if you want to heal, move forward and make your marriage work after the affair is over.

This book is also useful for people who are single and cheating with a married man or woman, the infamous third wheel. Not much has been written for you. In the following pages there is insight into why you are cheating, and some thoughts on what you can do about it.

This book can also help the one who's been cheated on, to gain insight into the cheater, but it's not been written directly for you. I would recommend other books as well, including *The New Monogamy: Redefining Your Relationship After Infidelity,* written more for you as the spouse and for those who are a couple.

This book also offers couples' therapists, sex therapists, clergy, and marriage counselors a look into the motivation behind complex affair relationships and the everyday people who have them.

Besides clinical advice, *When You're the One Who Cheats* includes real-life stories, narratives of people who have cheated and how things worked out for them, both positively and negatively. And how we can all relate to the desire for love and the craving to be loved.

Is This Book Pro-Affair or Anti-Affair?

As a board certified sexologist, certified therapist and licensed professional counselor with more than thirty years in the field of sex therapy, couples counseling, and infidelity treatment, I'm neither pro-affair nor anti-infidelity. I believe in creating sustainable relationships, and that integrity means honoring our commitments to ourselves and to others.

In my work I have been challenged with maintaining a nonbiased opinion about affairs. This has not always been easy. Especially when I have been personally affected by infidelity (as most of us have). In my first marriage, my ex-husband had an affair. This is not why my marriage broke up. In fact, I realized many years later, as I was standing on the dais of a large auditorium, lecturing to hundreds of marriage and family therapists and psychologists on the nature of infidelity and erotic recovery, that I was the one who colluded with my ex's infidelity. I had been the one to push them together. I had unconsciously, at the time, encouraged my ex-husband's affair with my best friend. I realized in the moment as I was speaking to this crowd of psychotherapists that I must have wanted my husband to know that he would be able to find a relationship once our marriage ended. And so I managed to find ways for him to spend time with my friend, a woman who I knew wanted to be with him. I am still amazed at my unconscious and unrealized collusion, and have only the deepest respect for the partners of those who cheat, for it is so easy to deny our own participation.

This is not to blame the victim in any way. Many times, as you will realize in reading this book, the partner and the marriage has nothing to do with an affair, which I also realized the hard way. Shortly after my divorce, I ended up in an affair with a married man. He was kind and caring and helped me through a lonely and difficult year. I was not concerned at the time that he had a wife. It didn't feel like I was cheating, it felt like he was the cheater, since he was married and I was not. It was only when I ran into his wife at a social event and realized that we might have been friends under different circumstances that I knew I couldn't keep up with the affair. I ended it.

What I learned from both of these experiences is that we are all people. People looking for love, for support; clearly, we are all just trying to make our lives work.

Today I am in a new, loving and long-term marriage. My husband and I have raised and launched four beautiful and successful children, and together we have made a life for ourselves beyond my wildest dreams. From this foundation, I have been able to pursue my mission in life which has become the search for truth and the sustainability in all relationships – this is the focus of my work and my writing.

And *I do not judge.*

Ashley Madison, a website for people who are married and looking for affairs, recently contacted me, wondering if I would be interested in acting as a consultant for them in the area of infidelity. When they had questions from the press, they wanted an expert in this area to speak about affairs, what they are, who has them and why. They wanted an expert who was not biased toward or against affairs. We talked about it for a long time before I agreed to speak as a consultant for them. I wondered how my role would be received. Would the public, my patients, my family, perceive me as someone who encouraged affairs, who supported infidelity? My husband and I discussed it for a long time.

I decided that the people being cheated on, those who are suffering after infidelity, and those that chose to cheat, had so much to say and not a lot of people helping them to say it. Affairs happen.

That's the truth.

I decided to tell the truth. Integrity, for me, is talking not only about the people who have been cheated on, but the ones that cheat.

Let's tell the truth about affairs, I thought.

People cheat.

I can help the cheaters tell the truth, and maybe this book can help them tell the truth about who they are, and what they really want.

Telling the truth about who you are is hard. But it's what creates real intimacy. It's also what makes relationships so damn painful.

The trouble with marriage today is that we don't tell the truth about it. Not really. We aren't being real about what's happening. Lots of people cheat. People get divorced. Let's start there and be honest about it. Will this book change infidelity? Definitely not. I'm not that powerful! But let's talk honestly about affairs, about cheating, and help not just the people who've been cheated on but the people who cheat, let's help *them* find a way to be honest – starting with being honest with themselves.

So what is the truth about relationships? About marriage? Telling the truth about who you are is painful. But it's the only real choice. Everything else is just fake news.

I hope that by writing this book, by being a voice for truth in the helping community, by standing up for integrity, I can stand up with - and for - those who are searching. Searching for wisdom, for understanding and for true love.

I recognize that integrity may be the greatest challenge of our time. What is the truth these days? Why do we focus on "false" news, "false" advertising, and lies? How do we, instead, begin to tell the truth when we need to? How do we believe it when we see it? What if the truth is not always easy?

In this book I hope you will find many ways to create a life where you can be true to yourself, to your agreements, even when, in fact, you have not been true to another person. I hope that standing up for your truth can mean living in integrity and healing your relationships at the same time.

Whether you are loyal to an outside relationship or an inside relationship, know that you also have a relationship with yourself, one that you will have to reconcile in order to move forward. This book will show you how to take those steps.

Will I See Myself in This Book?

When You're the One Who Cheats includes research, stories and interventions from my clinical practice, plus real-life experiences from individual cheaters and from couples seeking to recover from cheating, as well as from cheaters who have voluntarily contributed their stories. All of the names and details have been changed.

There are few books—if any—that provide the cheater with as much information to work through the intense feelings and difficult-to-make decisions that need to be made during this time in one's life. Forty to 60 percent of people will cheat at some point in their marriage, so know that you are not alone.

For those who aren't married but are cheating with someone who is, until now, there have been no books of advice out there for you and very little in the way of positive encouragement. You have been shamed, you have been disregarded and ignored: Your feelings have been treated as secondary and not important. As the outside partner you probably feel all of these things as well as feeling totally misunderstood. This can be quite lonely.[1]

The outside partner often gets left out of the narrative of cheating. This third person is sometimes treated as a throwaway, or sometimes as a unicorn, a kind of precious "other" who has the potential to significantly wake up a dead marriage and then, once the unicorn's work is done, is readily discarded. This book honors your place in the affair as well and looks to empower you to make choices that are best for you.

My hope is that, in reading this book, you will find that there's enough advice and encouragement for you to draw your own conclusions and make your own decisions, to understand your feelings and to gain insight into your future. You won't be judged. You may not find all the answers, but you may read things here that will make you think a lot—and maybe differently—about your infidelity.

---

1   *PLEASE NOTE: Some women are afraid of physical abuse if they refuse to comply with an affair or have sex with men in power. In this country and in others around the world, there are many women that are literally slaves to a system that keeps them in circumstances where they do not have choices about their sexual freedom. IMPORTANT: For the women who need more help than this book can provide: the women who are tortured and enslaved, used for sex against their will, or physically forced into the sex work trade, get out if you can. Call emergency services, and then seek legal intervention, therapy and political support. The internet is a great place to start your search - please find safety as soon as possible.*

CHAPTER ONE
You're the One Who Cheated

Cheater

OK, so you cheated. You're a cheater.

Being a cheater doesn't mean you're a terrible person. You have your reasons. You met someone. You were lonely. You fell in love. You were mad at your spouse. "It just happened." You don't believe in monogamy. It was only this *one* time. Your partner did it first. You love the excitement of extramarital sex and, well, "the sex is freaking amazing!"

Until it's not.

Your heart is breaking. You don't know what to do. You are out of your mind. You don't want to end your marriage. You want to keep your affair partner but think you should stop because you know you will never leave your spouse; or *they* will never leave their spouse. You told your spouse the affair was over but you lied. You can't live with yourself. You can't stop thinking about your affair partner. Your affair partner keeps calling and you're afraid you'll get caught. You've already been caught and have no idea what to do. You don't know why you did it/do it/want to do it again.

And you can't stop.

This book may not help you stop. But it will help you answer some of your biggest questions: Am I making a huge mistake? How do I deal with my guilt and shame? What do I do next?

And what about the rest of my life?

It is time to confront some of the more complicated issues:

Why did I cheat? Do I want to stay or go? Do I tell my spouse or not? Do I love my affair partner or am I staying for the sex?

Oh, and wait, what the hell have I done?

Sluts, Womanizers and Adulterers

First, forgive and accept the use of the term "cheater" throughout this book. Let's just get over the stigma now. Of course, the word "cheater" implies lots of terrible things. If you're a man, and a cheater, you may be called: *a bad guy, a philanderer, a womanizer, a Romeo, an adulterer, a lady killer, a Casanova, a rogue, a wife stealer, a sinner, a Judas, a scoundrel, a scallywag, a rascal, a scamp, a Don Juan, a player, a ladies' man, a heartbreaker, or an adulterer.*

If you're a woman, and a cheater, you may be accused of being: *a terrible wife, a seductress, a husband stealer, a home wrecker, a Mary Magdalene, a sinner, an adulteress, a flirt, a slut, a bitch, a prostitute, a whore, a whore bag, or even a whore's whore* (when someone's being really insulting). I'm sure I've missed some and you can think of lots of other names for cheaters.

You've probably never imagined being called any of these names, particularly if you're a woman. If you're a man, however, some of these epithets like "rogue" or "ladies' man" or "player" are considered flattering or compliments, and even worn like badges of honor. The terms applied to women, on the other hand, are—without exception—pejorative. It's a total double standard.

There's a movement these days to stop "slut shaming" women who enjoy sex with multiple partners or who own their sexuality. In our society it's not uncommon for both men and women to shame girls and adult women for their looks, their sensuality, their sexual behavior, their desires and/or their profession. In these pages, we'll have none of that. This isn't a book to shame or blame, particularly when it comes to sexual relationships. We're taking back the word "slut" so that it equates with a woman who is empowered in her own sexuality.

Let's do something similar with the word "cheater."

We're not doing this to license cheaters to continue cheating (that's totally up to you), but because there is nothing else to call you at this time. There's no other word for someone who breaks the bond of monogamy; nor a word that encompasses the role of the "other" in a cheating relationship.

For now, you're the *cheater*, and please don't cringe every time you read the word.

Own it. Unless you can think of a better word, that's what you are. Now let's move on because there's important stuff in the following pages that you need to know.

What is cheating?

Sometimes people have an implicit assumption that "texting affairs aren't cheating" or an "online affair—with no physical contact—isn't really infidelity." Or that an emotional affair isn't as much of a betrayal as a sexual affair. And, yet, at the heart of all betrayals are breaches of implicit assumptions about monogamy.

Often based on cultural mores, religious beliefs, traditional sex roles, family history, and personal morals and values, implicit assumptions may never be openly acknowledged or discussed.

Each partner may hold a different, sometimes opposite, understanding of the imposed limits of monogamy and therefore have wildly differing expectations. For example, to some, monogamy may include such implicit expectations as "strip clubs aren't a problem," or "posting nude selfies isn't infidelity" or "dirty dancing isn't cheating" or "mutual masturbation over the internet doesn't count" or "a little swinging on vacation is just fun, it's not a threat to our relationship."

Think about your implicit assumptions regarding your monogamy. How much have you actually discussed with your partner? Did you have an open conversation with your spouse when you got married?

Not many couples promise to love, honor and tell each other absolutely everything. What are the rules when you get married? Should you tell each other when you have a new friend on social media, or when you're thinking about someone else or when you masturbate in the shower? Should you tell every detail to your partner of what's in your mind if it involves a fantasy of someone else? Does your partner want to know?

Negotiating the contours of your monogamy is an important part of making a relationship work. *Do you talk about the things that should be explicit in your monogamy?* This doesn't mean you have to share *every* single thing you think or do. But you might assume what this means to your partner. And you may be wrong.

What is private and what is secret? Should you tell your spouse every time you go to lunch or talk on the phone with a friend? A conversation about implicit assumptions about everyday behaviors can be even more important than the vows that you make at your wedding.

Whether you've decided to stay married and make your marriage work, or leave your spouse and work on your next relationship, making your implicit monogamy assumptions explicit is a skill you'll need to master to have any sustainable partnership going forward. Creating a new monogamy is an important goal if you want to start over, either with your current partner or someone new.

Cheating today is different than it's ever been. We can cheat on our partner lying in bed next to them, on our handheld devices. There's never been a time when finding someone to cheat with has been so easy and finding ways to do it so prevalent. This could be one reason why the rates of infidelity are so high today. The estimates for extramarital affairs in the United States say that between 20 to 40 percent of all people will cheat at some point in their marriage.[i]

Men have traditionally bragged about their affairs and women have downplayed their infidelity, even to researchers collecting information, so we don't know if these rates are accurate. But it makes sense that with the ease of finding partners on the internet and the types of cheating available, more people than ever are exploring affairs. We also live longer than ever before so, although we are expected to be desirous of one person for the duration of our married life, monogamy is more difficult and less enticing than it was when we lived shorter lives two hundred years ago.

Married but Dating

As an exploratory exercise, and to do research for this book, I logged onto one of the more popular "married but dating" websites, Ashley Madison, a website where married people meet other married people to have an affair. There are 54 million people worldwide on the website, and I wanted to know what was drawing so many people to the cheating site.

I created a couple of profiles for myself. I wanted to know and understand what the experience was like to cheat online. I was also curious about how it might be different for men and for women, and for gay and for straight people.

First, I created a profile as a man looking to date a married woman and loaded it with as little information as possible. I didn't say anything about what kind of woman I was looking for, and I did not post a photo. I did the same thing posting a profile as a woman looking for a man.

As a man—let's call my male profile persona "Tom" —I was six foot two inches and two hundred pounds. As a woman, I was "Tina," at five foot eight and one hundred and forty pounds. All within normal range, if a little on the tall side.

I also set up a profile as a woman, "Tara," seeking a woman.

I wanted to see what the overall experience looked like and felt like for both genders. I didn't purchase credits to speak with any other members and I didn't respond to anyone who messaged or winked at me. The experience was purely for observation, like peering into a fish bowl without being able to swim with the fish. I didn't want to misrepresent myself to anyone on the site as being available to date, since I was purely interested in responses to my profile. I purposely never winked, sent messages or expressed interest in any of the men or women on the site.

But I have to say I was interested.

The first few days my profile was up as a woman seeking a man, I received over 130 messages and 190 winks, right away. I got lots of photos. And they kept coming, even if I didn't respond to them. The men sent me private messages and keys to unlock more intimate information about themselves. They pursued me, even though I didn't have a photo or a description of myself. I was a fantasy, I thought… a blank canvas onto which to project their extramarital dreams.

These men seeking women for an affair sent me interesting messages. The majority of them surprised me with their content. They were looking for relationships outside of their marriage, they were clear about that. They didn't want to break up their marriages. But they wanted a connected relationship, they didn't just want sex. As one guy put it, "*I want more than just a f**k buddy.*"

Most of the men were looking for companions, for someone to spend time with, "*inside and outside the bedroom.*" They claimed they lacked "*intimacy*" and "*attention*" at home and they wanted to find someone "*passionate about [spending] time together.*" They were "*looking for a companion to enjoy the best of what life and a new relationship has to offer.*"

What are these men looking for in an extramarital

relationship? They seem to be turned on by the idea of a getaway, and are eager to shake things up. *"We could escape our boring lives together!"* and *"I am looking to add some excitement to a stale routine."* But more often they want someone to *"talk to,"* and,*" text…every day."* They're looking for something consistent, a partnership that is a parallel to their companionship at home. *"Maybe we can be friends,"* one stranger insisted.

A few seemed to be looking for revenge because someone had cheated on them. They seemed wounded; they wanted someone *"honest,"* that they could *"trust,"* that would be *"open"* with them.

But what was most surprising is that all of the men seemed to have this same craving—someone to connect with, *"both mentally and physically."* They were *"not into one-night stands or quickies."*

They wanted *"intelligent conversation,"* and *"long dinners out,"* and, in general, a *"long-term side relation-ship."* One guy described it well when he said he was *"looking for one woman to have an ongoing love affair, in and out of the bedroom."* Another wrote*: "I am not look-ing for a hookup, but a lasting relationship."* And another said, *"I am not really into a one-time thing."*

This seems to go against the popular idea that men cheat for sex and women cheat for emotional connection and relationship. The men that contacted me were clear that they were seeking what they no longer had at home: "*passion, desire, lust, kink, romance.*" But they wanted it to build up over time. Some of the men were clear that they didn't want to rush into sex. "*I want to get to know you before we just jump into bed,*" said one middle-aged guy, clearly looking for love.

Given that this is a small, self-selected sample of men between 40 and 65, it could be a reflection of age, and mechanics. Middle-aged sex works better when there is a gradual buildup of arousal. The men said things like "*Sex works best when I am emotionally and intellectually connected,*" and, "*I am happy to let things move slowly,*" and "*I would prefer to let a relationship develop over time.*"

And the men seemed nice. They went out of their way to assure me they were not into "*anything painful or weird,*" and they were not a "*weirdo*" or a "*stalker type*" and they weren't into anything "*scary.*"

I was most struck by the longing in their messages. The lack of penis photos. The craving for passion and connection. I wouldn't have guessed that men seeking an affair would be so blatantly clear that they wanted a relationship, not just sex. And, if you think about it, that makes sense. They could go to a sex worker if all they wanted was a quickie. But where else would they go for a relationship when they didn't want to leave their wife? A married but dating website.

And then there was my Tom persona profile. I didn't get as many responses to this account and the messages dropped off quickly when I didn't respond to them. What struck me immediately about the females was the photos. While the male photos were all men with boats, men with motorcycles, men with fish, and men with dogs, the women's photos were blurred headless shots of naked legs and boobs. The women were much more forward, and at times a tad poetic, *"I would like a man to ease my loneliness with his muscular thighs,"* and their posts contained brazen messages of desire; *"[let's] indulge in wanton debauchery."*

The women wanted sex. They wanted oral sex and threesomes and sex toys, and they wanted it steamy and quick and they wanted it when the kids were off at school and they did not want a relationship. They wanted a one-time thing. They wanted a stranger. They wanted parking lots and hotel rooms and anonymity. The women who responded were clear that they were not looking for a committed partner.

One woman said, *"I don't want to hear about the*

problems in your marriage. Don't tell me about your terrible job. You have a wife for that. I want hot sex and then...well, get out."

The women were very direct about the kind of sex they were interested in. Maybe it's the influence of the bestselling book *Fifty Shades of Grey*, but the women who responded to my profile defined themselves as "*a tad deviant,*" and they wanted a man who was interested in "*blindfolds and paddles and...pinwheels and crops and handcuffs.*"

Most had no interest in lovemaking. They wanted communication, yes, but communication about "*...what [you're] going to do to me tonight.*" Some women wanted a man who was "*adventurous*" or "*kinky.*" Or "*daring... in public.*" They were looking for "*...a man who isn't afraid to be a little rough with me in bed,*" and "*a man who follows his instinct and his desire*"—a man who is "*spontaneous.*"

Some sent lingerie poses and pursued me, sending photos and messages until it was clear I wasn't going to respond. Then they ghosted. I got no winks. I read a message from one woman who liked "*being fingered while...*" but the rest of her desires were deleted, perhaps by a website monitor. Although she later disguised her particular wants as liking: "*Prince Albert.*"

What surprised me about the response to the man seeking a woman was how many of the women were clearly looking for sex, and for sex only. They didn't want a relationship, they weren't looking for love, they had no interest in a long-term parallel partnership. They wanted something naughty, something illicit, something hot. This goes against many of the standard ideas about why women cheat.

Woman Seeking Woman

In my profile as a woman seeking a woman, I received very few responses. Of the messages I did receive, only about 30 percent were from women looking for a lesbian relationship. The other 70 percent were from bisexual or bi-curious women seeking another woman for a three-some. Some were clear that the partner was involved in creating the online profile: "*sexy couple looking for adventuresome female to join for fun & play,*" and "*really looking to explore fantasies with another couple,*" "*want to try being with another woman,*" and "*you can bring your husband to watch or to join us.*"

Most of the female seeking female profiles had clear photos of the woman in lingerie, many of them in a bra and panties. There were several profiles of women that simply said: "*...searching for a woman to play alone or* *as two couples*."

I wondered, where do the lesbians go to meet other women to have an affair? Maybe lesbians don't cheat as often? The research is inconclusive.

My takeaway from my experiment as a cheater online is that we are wrong about why men and women cheat. Married men want passion and relationships. And women want sex; hot and sometimes kinky sex. This says that we cannot explain affairs by antiquated ideas, or biased beliefs about gender. Our stereotyped narratives of female and male cheating don't explain individualized experiences, wants, and desires.

In other words, the reason you cheated can't be explained by your gender or your sexual orientation. It's more complicated than that. And in the end, it may not matter if you fit into a category at all. What matters is what you can do about it.

What Do We Know?

Online cheating leads to real-time relationships about 30 percent of the time. By the time you've gone online to find a partner to have an affair, you have made up your mind that you are looking for infidelity.

Websites for married people to date other married people, sites like "Ashley Madison" and the website

"Marital Affairs"—social media websites that clearly state members are there to meet other married members—provide the opportunity for both men and women to seek out exactly what they are looking for: a dalliance, extramarital sex and/or a long-term affair. These online cheating websites provide an equalizing choice experience. Sites like these level the playing field for women. Online married dating is a way for women to have as much power as men, to choose—to pick a partner based on looks and sexual attraction. Women don't have to wait to be asked out on a date. They choose a partner on the site based solely on a profile and decide if they want to take the relationship off the website and meet in person. If they are attracted, they get to decide if that means having sex. For women, the power of married dating can bring back a waning self-esteem and restore a sense of free will.

Wednesday Martin, author of *UNTRUE: Why Nearly Everything We Believe About Women, Lust, and Infidelity Is Wrong and How the New Science Can Set Us Free*[ii] says that, "much of what we've been taught about female sexuality is untrue...many experts now believe that the female libido, when measured correctly, is every bit as strong as the male."

Whether you are a man or a woman, gay or straight

or bisexual, don't assume that you or your partner(s) will behave in a way that is traditionally ascribed to a certain role. Cheating has no boundaries.

Your Explicit Monogamy Agreement

Monogamy, a legal term, means to be married to one person. In our culture, the explicit monogamy agreement's primary function is the promise of sexual fidelity to a partner in marriage. We don't need a legal agreement to have children, to purchase property, or to have sex. The motivation these days is emotional. (Unless, for some, it's for citizenship, health or life insurance, or to share or pass on property.)

The explicit monogamy agreement is basically a promise you make out loud, a vow in front of family and friends, in a church or a synagogue—it's the words you state clearly about loving, honoring and cherishing only one another. The agreement is generally considered to be your marriage vows, part of your commitment ceremony, your lifelong pledge.

You also sign a legal document in front of witnesses. The document is then filed in the county office. That document is meant to bind the two of you together for life so that you can share things as mentioned earlier: life insurance, health insurance, or a mortgage. It makes you mutually responsible for your children, and eligible to inherit one another's wealth upon death. It also makes you responsible for shared financial debts.

The explicit monogamy agreement also—usually—promises fidelity. You promise not to sleep with anyone else except each other, 'til death do you part.

We take this promise of monogamy quite seriously, even though we know we can break this explicit agreement at any time. Everyone knows it's not really legal to sexually obligate each other to *only* one another, right?

I bet when you got married and you made this explicit monogamy agreement, you meant every word (kind of). But you also knew you could get out of it, if you wanted. Fifty percent of people do. And lots of other people who stay married cheat.

The explicit monogamy agreement idea is actually a somewhat antiquated tradition. It's sweet. But it's certainly not binding.

Yet we still believe in it, even if we don't necessarily uphold it. We love and cherish the idea of it. And we don't like to think that *we* couldn't make it work. While researching infidelity, author Pamela Druckerman[iii] found that more than 80 percent of respondents to her survey about affairs said that infidelity was *wrong*. Of those who admitted to cheating, a majority didn't think of themselves as the "cheating kind." No one, it appears, likes to think of themselves as a "cheater."

None of us want to identify as the kind of person who could be unfaithful. We prefer to think that's what "other" people do. In fact, in America, people think cheating is worse than polygamy *and* human cloning.[iv]

When we make an explicit vow, we believe we'll honor that promise.

Until we don't.

Peggy Vaughan, author of *The Monogamy Myth,*[v] wrote: "Saying 'I do' is supposed to be a one-time promise to prevent a lifetime of infidelity." But that's like saying: "I told you I loved you when I married you. I'll let you know if anything changes." The vow itself is not the thing that keeps you faithful.

When you cheated, you broke this explicit monogamy agreement—you broke the promise, you broke your vow. You knew what you were doing. You knew you were breaking your vow while you were doing it. So, take responsibility for your choice. No one made you do it. No one made you cross the line.

Want some more bad news? You didn't just end an agreement. You ended your marriage—*right at that moment*, when you crossed the line and began your affair—because your monogamy agreement *is* the marriage. You broke your promise and *ended your contract*.

Don't waste time trying to navigate around the reality by denying or justifying it. You did it, so own it.

Now let's figure out how you should proceed.

Stop Blaming Your Partner

You want to figure out why you cheat(ed) and what to do about it. To begin, you need to stop blaming everyone else for your behavior. A lot of cheaters blame their spouse for their affair—otherwise known as "blaming the victim." Put an end to that right now. No more blaming your spouse, or your parents, or your addiction, or your therapist.

As the cheater, it's time to own your behavior. You have your needs, you have your wants, and you have your affair(s). No one else is to blame for what you did.

Implicit Monogamy Agreement

The implicit monogamy agreement is the unspoken understanding that you *think* you have with your spouse about how fidelity in your marriage works. We all have assumptions about monogamy, many of which are based on our family history, on our experiences, and on our culture. But we rarely discuss these implicit monogamy assumptions with our partners, even (or especially) if we suspect, for instance, that our spouse might disagree with some of the finer points of these assumptions.

One common and unspoken implicit monogamy assumption is that "all men cheat."

Rob, a client of mine, got married at thirty-one. His explicit monogamy agreement was clear. On the day they married he told his wife, Helen, that he would never sleep with anyone else. She looked into his eyes and vowed that she would never cheat on him either. One year to the day after they married, Rob and Helen came to my office for a couple's therapy session.

Rob had slept with a girl he met at a bar while Helen was away on business. Helen was angry about the infidelity and what she said was Rob's "lackadaisical" attitude about the affair.

"He thinks it's no big deal, sleeping with this woman," she said. "He says it's, like, what guys do!"

Rob looked at me, one arm draped over the back of the sofa. He lifted his chin, as if daring me to challenge the statement. I asked him, instead: "What did this affair mean to you Rob?"

"First," he said, "This was not an affair, it was a one-night stand, and it meant nothing. I don't even know the girl's name. It wasn't anything to me, so it should be nothing to Helen."

Helen stared at him blankly.

I asked Rob what his father thought of cheating. "My father took me to my first prostitute when I was fifteen," he said. "To... you know, lose my virginity. All the guys in my family went. It's no big deal."

"So, Rob," I said, "It seems like your implicit assumption about cheating is that 'all guys do it' and, as long as there's no emotional connection, then it's no big deal, right?"

He nodded his head in agreement.

"But this is not Helen's implicit assumption about monogamy."

Helen said, "No! Sex with another person is cheating. I assumed that when we got married you wouldn't do it with anyone but me. I don't care if you've been doing this since you were fifteen."

I asked Rob and Helen if they'd had a conversation about their monogamy assumptions prior to their wedding. Neither of them had thought to bring it up. Each had assumed the other knew how they felt about monogamy, with Rob assuming his pre-marital behavior could continue as long as Helen didn't know about it. "That's the way the men in my family did it; they didn't tell their wives."

Helen and Rob ultimately agreed that their monogamy could be different from their parents' monogamy. A longer conversation was necessary to decide what was important to each of them in a marriage. They realized then that they could and would need to renegotiate their monogamy agreement, to make it work for them, in order to stay together and be happy.

Denial

Most cheaters justify the idea in their head before they cheat. Building a case, they start to add up all of the things wrong with their marriage, and with their partner. If they aren't already fighting, they start to pick arguments with their spouse. (Note: For the rest of the book the term "spouse" will be used interchangeably with the term "primary partner" or "committed partner" to indicate the person you are cheating on, or have cheated on.)

When you build up enough resentment, enough emotional ammunition, it becomes easier to consciously justify the decision to cheat.

This is crucial: you need to get out of the "denial" mode. Unless you were in a total alcoholic blackout, or "roofied," you knew you were cheating. (If you think you were unknowingly drugged, get help immediately. If you don't remember what you did because you were in an alcohol or drug-induced "fugue state," then you need to get tested for STDs. Then consider an alcohol or drug treatment center. It's time.)

Take responsibility for your actions. You didn't just fall into bed with this person. There are no accidental affairs. The old "it just happened" excuse is a way to avoid ownership of your behavior and a way to romanticize the impulsiveness of your affair.

The reality is this: you knew, at the moment you crossed the line, that you were breaking your monogamy agreement. You committed to your primary partner—you said you wouldn't cheat. And despite the seeming impulsivity of the affair, you had some time for contemplation before you did it.

You spent time flirting with the idea and maybe with the person you wanted to have the affair with. You may have spent weeks thinking about whether or not you should do it. Or your time of contemplation might have even been months or sometimes, even years.

So, yes, the decision to cheat usually comes well before the actual cheating. Once the decision has been made, then you start looking. You create the opportunity. Even if you tell yourself the cheating is impulsive. Even if the affair happens in the heat of the moment. Even if you spontaneously connect with your ex on social media, or you pop into a local massage parlor for the first time, or you download porn for just for a quick peek. Even if it feels wholly spontaneous, if you stop and honestly consider what you were thinking prior to cheating, you may find that, "Yes, I had been thinking about doing this for quite a while." It's rare for people to cheat without some prior consideration and without any forethought or planning.

Endnotes

i   Atkins, Baucom, & Jacobson, 2001; Lauman, Gagnon, Michael, & Michaels, 1994

ii   Martin, Wednesday, 2018, Untrue: Why Nearly Everything We Believe About Women, Lust, and Infidelity Is Wrong and How the New Science Can Set Us Free, Little, Brown Spark, NY, NY

iii Drukerman, Pamela, 2008 in *Lust in Translation: Infidelity from Tokyo to Tennessee* Penguin Books; Reprint edition

iv   Drukerman, *Lust in Translation: Infidelity from Tokyo to Tennessee*

v   Vaughan, Peggy, 2009, *The Monogamy Myth,* Newmarket Press; Third Edition, Harper Collins Publishers, NY, NY

CHAPTER TWO
It Doesn't Matter Why You Did It

Emily Brown, in her book *Patterns of Infidelity and Their Treatment*[vi] says that "Love and betrayal, those powerful and human themes, are most dramatic in the extramarital affair. Affairs and the emotions they arouse have been described over the centuries in literature, history, and religion. Works of art depict scenes of the unfaithful. Modern tales are told in movies, song, and other media. Both old and new tales recount great passions and deadly secrets, deep love and idyllic illusions, pain and punishment, and, in some cases, redemption and healing. With such great drama, it is no wonder that now, as in the past, affairs capture everyone's interest."

And yet, when an affair is the center of your life, it can be painful and perplexing, exciting, yes, but confusing. Why is it happening to you?

Why Do People Cheat?

Affairs happen. People break their monogamy agreements

for lots of reasons. If you're the cheater, you've probably googled any or all of the following:

> *Affairs; Infidelity; Cheating; Why am I cheating? Should I end my affair? Should I stop cheating; How to stop cheating; Infidelity; Extramarital affairs; When you're the one who cheats; I can't stop cheating; Will they ever leave their spouse for me? Why do people lie? Should I tell? Should I leave my spouse, and; How do I tell if my cellphone is bugged?*

Most likely you've searched for answers in the middle of the night on your laptop or your phone, combing through solutions and suggestions from the great oracle that is Google. Sitting up in bed, with your partner sleeping next to you, you've tapped out your most pressing questions, your deep philosophical wonderings, things you should really only talk to your therapist about.

If you have a therapist.

You've probably read all the blog posts, the online articles, and the free advice by experts who told you definitively that there are "three reasons people cheat" or "women cheat for fifteen reasons…" or "there is only one reason men cheat."

As one of those experts, I have written hundreds of those articles and blog posts, and I can tell you that there are as many reasons for cheating as there are people who cheat. The reasons do tend to fall into categories, and it's easy to lump the reasons together. But don't get too hung up on finding the one single reason that defines why you cheat. It doesn't matter so much why you cheated.

Worry more about the story of your affair. What did/ does it mean to you? In your life? In your marriage? And how did/does it make you feel about yourself?

How Do You Define an Affair?

How we define an affair today is not as straightforward as you may think. Technology and the internet have complicated our notion of what infidelity is by making intimacy with anyone, anywhere, easy and accessible. Is it cheating if we never physically meet with the other person? What if we never touch them or never see their photo or never even learn their name?

Is it cheating if it's only texting or phone sex? What if we do it while lying in bed next to our spouse?

An Affair Has Three Parts

To make it clear, I've broken down the definition of an affair into three parts: The Outside Relationship. The

Sexual Infidelity, and The Dishonesty.

All affairs can be divided into three parts:
1. The outside relationship
2. The sexual infidelity
3. The dishonesty

1) The Outside Relationship

An affair involves a relationship with someone outside of the primary partnership or marriage. It can be with a sex worker, or with someone you've met online but never in person. The relationship can be with a friend or colleague, an old college drinking buddy, an ex-lover, or an ex-spouse that you occasionally meet for lunch or dinner. It can be a one-night stand or it can be an ongoing love affair.

Sometimes the outside relationship is a parallel marriage; a long-time affair that has led to children and a second home. Some couples have long-lasting affairs, living parallel lives, maintaining two separate relationships, sometimes for as long as twenty years, or even more.

In our culture, intimacy and loyalty are often reserved entirely for the spouse. Within this model any kind of sharing of thoughts or feelings or time spent with others outside of the dyad (couple) relationship—including any loving feelings shared with a close friend—may be considered a threat to the marriage.

Sharing intimate thoughts and secrets with a friend or a stranger online can be interpreted as a type of theft from the marriage's "closed door" emotional monogamy. These outside relationships can be collegial, romantic, or solely based on sexual attraction. They can be male to male or female to female. And they can be relationships that share work, travel, hobbies, food, or social or political connections. Any relationship that offers a visual or intellectual intimacy can lead to this type of infidelity.

Cheating occurs on a continuum and when it comes to the outside relationship affair, it can be an act of *curiosity* only, or it can be more of a *fantasy,* which sometimes develops into *action.*

For instance, on one end of the spectrum of monogamy, the notion of "coveting" thy neighbor's wife or "lusting" after another "in your heart" (as President Jimmy Carter once put it) are examples of fantasizing about a relationship outside marriage. For those being "cheated on," and who hold strong beliefs about the sanctity of their marriage, just the act of "thinking" about cheating can feel like betrayal—and may signal the beginning of a slippery slope leading to more complicated cheating behavior.

For others, the emotional connection with a friend or co-worker can turn from simple friendship into an emotional affair.

The Work Spouse

Some people have what I call a work spouse; an office mate they spend more time with during the week than they do with their spouse. Office mates share the everyday ups and downs and, at times, personal and private experiences that create an emotional bond.

Some colleagues eventually form a "vicinity attraction." A vicinity attraction happens when you develop a strong connection with a colleague because of the many hours you spend on projects or in tight quarters. If you travel together for work you share both stressful and rewarding experiences. You have many interests in common—which makes sense. You probably have similar educational backgrounds if you are in the same field, and are concerned with the same social or political issues. You may even have the same global concerns.

You look forward to talking daily and sharing stories about work and home. You help each other deal with work stress and tension by talking things through. Eventually, you think of them outside of work and yearn to connect with them. You want to talk about things affecting not just your work life, but your personal life as well.

You might even grow curious about their time spent away from work, and begin to search for them on social media.

It's never been easier to seek out or "stalk" our colleagues: to google their private lives, to check out what they like to do and where they like to go when they aren't at work. We can check out their families, follow their dates, see where they're eating and what they look like in relaxed settings. We see them on vacation, in casual clothes and in bathing suits. And we know who their friends are.

It's easy to become intimately connected to our work friends outside of our work lives. In an instant we're messaging, then texting, then calling each other on the phone. Finally, things escalate to meeting outside work hours for lunch or drinks. It makes sense that the work-spouse relationship can so easily become more.

The work-spouse relationship is certainly not the only kind of emotional affair, but it is a common one.

2) Sexual Infidelity

Another important part of an affair is the sexual infidelity—it's also the most titillating and, at the same time, the most fraught aspect of an affair. (Again, infidelity occurs on a continuum and isn't necessarily limited to the physical act of sexual intercourse.)

Most people would have no argument with the declaration that sex outside the marriage is cheating. But would they agree that viewing porn, or masturbating to erotic imagery, or having a cyber relationship with someone online (in which no touching occurs), is also cheating?

Does it count if the other person is an online sexual partner and is only flirting? And if they take their clothes off while online, is that a sexual affair? What constitutes sexual infidelity?

Arnie and Pete had been together for twenty years. They came to therapy because Arnie thought that his cheating didn't count because his infidelities were only online, with paid sex workers. Pete had had no idea that Arnie saw these sex workers on a regular basis. Arnie had always believed that "this is what all gay men do, we see people on the side." But that was his implicit assumption. He never spoke with Pete about this belief nor did he ask him how he felt about it. When Pete discovered that Arnie was hiring sex workers, even "just" for virtual sex online, he felt betrayed and angry.

During one session in my office, Pete said to Arnie,

"If you weren't sexually satisfied, you could have just told me. I would have tried harder; we could have talked about it."

"Pete, please," Arnie said, "I didn't want to hurt your feelings. I know I want sex more often than you do and I want a different kind of sex. I just want casual sex. No emotion. I figured it was on the internet, I never met these guys, it wasn't even real. It shouldn't interfere with our relationship."

"If we had talked about it," Pete replied, "maybe I could have agreed. But we never had the conversation. You never gave me a chance to have it as part of our understanding."

In the end, Pete decided that he was fine with Arnie seeing sex workers, as long as he kept it virtual and didn't plan to meet anyone in real life and didn't lie about it when asked. It was the secrecy that Pete felt threatened by. He said he preferred the idea of Arnie engaging with paid sex workers over the internet, masturbating with a webcam, rather than engaging in a real-time sex or an emotional affair with another man.

"I don't want to risk Arnie falling in love with someone else. This way he's happy and I don't have to worry. I know he'll keep his emotional walls up with someone he isn't touching and with someone he is paying for sex. If he can still be passionate and feel like he's having some fun, then it's okay. As long as I don't have to be afraid that he's going to leave me for someone else."

Arnie said, "And yes, I can do this on the nights when Pete goes to bed early, if he isn't into having sex."

Pete added, "Yes and now I guess I don't have to feel guilty if I'm not meeting all of Arnie's sexual needs."

Sex Workers

Sex with a paid sex worker *is* cheating for couples who define cheating as *any* kind of sex outside of the relationship, with *any* other person. (Note: Sex worker, not "prostitute," is the preferred term. "Prostitute" is a dated and loaded term while "sex worker" acknowledges the work that is an exchange of services for money, rather than the social status the old term implies. Read more at: https://inews.co.uk/opinion/columnists/sex-workers-prostitutes-words-matter/)

Sex workers of both genders are paid for a wide variety of sexual acts. If your massage therapist, for instance, gives you a "happy ending," he or she is a sex worker, and this could be considered cheating.

You may think that a one-time indiscretion with a sex worker doesn't count; that it's not as devastating to a marriage as a long-term, emotional affair. And you may think you can keep that one-time infidelity hidden. Maybe you think you can forget it altogether.

Some people do keep incidents like these compartmentalized, closed off from the rest of their lives. They're able to shut such an episode down, stuffed away in a mental box, allowing them to live their life as if it never happened. The one-time sexual indiscretion is kept secret, separated from their real lives.

Even cheaters who have ongoing contact with a sex worker are sometimes able to keep these affairs contained so the experience never intrudes on their emotional relationships at home. They don't see the conflict of having both a marriage partner and a paid sexual partner on the side, particularly if there's little or no emotional connection and it doesn't seem to interfere with their primary love relationship.

If there is a sexual relationship *of any kind* outside of your marriage or primary relationship, *and you haven't agreed to an open relationship* with your spouse, then it's cheating. It's that simple.

Whether cheating with a sex worker affects you or your partner or your relationship is not something this book can decide for you. That is something you have to consider and decide for yourself.

What Are You Expecting?

As a certified sex and relationship therapist, I've met hundreds of couples who believe that the passion is gone from their relationship; and each individual blames their partner for the lack of passion. They sit on my couch and say, "If you can just fix him/her, we'd be fine." Usually there's a "desire discrepancy"—one person wants sex more than the other. Or they want to explore a different kind of sex. Or they've lost sexual interest in the other partner entirely.

I hear both sides of the story.

You may have an expectation that, after decades of marriage, your spouse's desire will be undiminished, even though—according to your spouse—you've stopped doing many of the things that made them desire you in the first place.

At the start of a relationship you flirt, you seduce, you entertain, you make your partner feel sexy. You feel sexy. The sex is good and you feel real desire for each other.

But, after years together, you may no longer think about walking in the door after work and making love immediately your partner. You may both be both cranky because you've put in ten hours at the office, and you still have to walk the dog and get the kids to bed. Besides, neither of you may be contributing anything new or exciting to the relationship. The reality of married life is that most partners work and have overarching responsibilities. So spontaneous, exciting sex may happen less often and both partners may feel less satisfied.

And, now that you're cheating, you've been swept off your feet by your affair partner. That makes sense —you and your affair partner have been putting in the effort to make the affair work. You're grooming more, dressing with care, and regularly sending sexy texts. In the affair, you are creating the opportunity and the desire for spontaneous sex. Therefore, it is happening often, or all the time.

People Cheat Because It Makes Them Feel Wanted

People cheat for lots of reasons, not the least of which is that they like the way it feels. Being wanted, feeling desired, having someone make us feel special—these are all fantastic feelings. Being a "lover" is exactly as romantic as it sounds. It's being swept off your feet, being adored, and feeling special.

Women who cheat, for instance, report that their lovers make them feel special, sexy, and adored, and *that* kind of attention is hard to ignore.

Gigi has been married to her husband for nineteen years. She is 44 and he is 50. They have no children, out of mutual agreement. She's a designer who regularly goes on buying trips to Milan, Paris, and Rome. Her husband, Roy, is in agriculture and needs to be on a farm year-round to maintain a crop of soy beans and oversee the processing plant. They live in the Midwest, where they grew up, and vacation with their extended families. On the surface, Gigi seems happy though Roy seems less so.

Gigi found a way to make herself happy: she was cheating to stay married. In a recent interview, Gigi told me that she had met multiple men on Ashley Madison, and currently had three boyfriends. Her husband had no idea about the cheating and she wanted to keep it that way.

Gigi spoke every day with the three men, by text or phone. And she talked to other men as well. She "didn't realize how unsatisfied" she was in her marriage until she met the first man she cheated with. After that it became clear that she would need to find her sexual satisfaction outside of marriage.

"Once I realized the level of attractiveness I had for my sexual partners, and they for me, it became the driving impetus; until then, my physical needs weren't being met at home. There was no longer any physical attraction between my husband and me. I wanted more, I wanted different, I wanted new."

I challenged the idea of her husband being in the dark about her affairs. Janis Spring, author of *After the Affair*, told me in an interview that, "After forty years of working as a therapist with people recovering from affairs, I can tell you that *usually* the person having the affair gets found out. People cheating aren't thinking. You are free to be with the other person, of course, but treat your partner with respect, tell them the truth. Be thoughtful. What do you want to happen?"

I asked Gigi this question: "What do you want to happen?" She said that she'd tried to bring up the subject of divorce with her husband but that he had become agitated and upset. And she realized that the work, the time, the cost of a divorce was too hard. She didn't want to hurt her husband that way. She would rather continue with what she was doing. She had a busy life, as did he, and she didn't feel guilty. She quoted the artist Vincent Van Gogh, "*I'd rather die of passion than of boredom.*"

"I'd rather die of passion than of boredom."

- Vincent Van Gogh.

Gigi said, "I'm having fun, enjoying myself."

I asked Gigi if she had any advice for other cheaters out there who would be reading this book. She immediately said, "Enjoy yourself! And stop if you feel guilty."

I asked how she managed all three of the men she was dating. Did she tell them about each other? How did that work? And was she having sex with all three of them? Had she ever done it with more than one of them at the same time? Was she emotionally attached to them? To one or more? Could she see herself leaving her husband for any one of them?

She told me that she would "never be physically intimate" with someone she didn't like. And that they were "all great people." She had sex with each of them, but never together and no, she didn't tell any of them about the rest of her life, or what she was doing, or who she was seeing. It was none of their business.

When I asked her about the vision for her future, she said, "If I do get divorced, I will never get married again. I would only pursue boyfriends because, in doing that, I'd never be bored and I don't want to be bored. I don't want to cheat again on a husband. There was a time, when sex with my husband was good, but that went away. I'd be afraid that a second marriage would end up the same. If I was single again, I'd only date and sleep with people. I wouldn't get permanently attached to anyone."

Gigi has changed and grown as a person since she started cheating. She is less introverted, she said, and more outgoing, friendly, confident, *and* more excited about life. Sensitive and sympathetic, she still cares for her husband. But her husband's conflict-avoidant personality, his unwillingness to discuss their relationship, has made it easier to cheat and ignore any issues in their marriage. Although his behavior made it difficult to improve their marriage, it made it easy for Gigi to find sexual fulfillment, to discover the erotic part of herself, and to understand her own sexual needs. And cheating, she felt, has made her a better person, ironically, a more fulfilled and vibrant woman.

Seeking Sexual Satisfaction

There's no denying that affair sex can be great. The excitement, spontaneity and passion of a new relationship means that it might be very different from the sex you're having with your committed partner.

And if things aren't going so well at home, and you don't have a great sex life—or any sex life—with your spouse, why wouldn't you consider straying?

We know from research that seeking sexual satisfaction is one of the key reasons that people look for an affair partner.

But, before you cheat, could you create more sexual satisfaction and increase the passion at home? Janis

Spring[vii] believes that "The hurt person [or spouse] can never compete with the fantasy of the affair person. Even the affair [partner] can't compete with the fantasy of the affair [partner]." People are swept up with the fantasy, a projection of the affair, and the cheaters believe they'll be happy. Spring says, "It's like going to the Ritz Carlton, but just for the weekend." These relationships fail at as high a rate as many marriages, if not higher.

People cheat when they find a man or a woman who turns them on and gives them the sex or relationship they want. Good sex, erotic sex, hot sex is arousing, life-affirming, and yes, sometimes hard to duplicate in a long-term relationship. When a couple has been together for years, or when they are new to each other but can't effectively communicate their needs in bed, finding an affair partner who just "gets it" can be a temporary relief. This can be hard to duplicate in a long-term relationship.

Most people want awe inspiring sex. And it's not just men who want good sex. If anyone tells you that men cheat for sex and women cheat for emotion, they're wrong—though they may be forgiven for being either naïve, sexist, or just out of touch with reality. Women cheat for sex, just as men do, and appreciate good sex as much as anyone. In fact, women aged eighteen to twenty-nine commit adultery more often than men do. Given the age bracket, this could be what I call the "hot momma" phenomenon. When a young mother finds someone who makes her feel less like a mommy and more like she used to feel—like a hot, sexy single woman—the invitation to cheat can be hard to turn down.

If you're elbow deep in macaroni and cheese and soccer cleats, finding a lover who makes you feel sexually appealing and erotic can be quite tempting. For some women, it's even worth the risk of losing their husbands, their families and, sometimes, their dignity. Cheating can make you feel exciting and desirable.

When a husband sees you only as your child's caregiver, as the breast feeder/food supplier, or, if after childbirth he no longer treats you as a sexual being, having a lover can reassure you that you still have that attractiveness that makes you more than just a wife or a mother.

3) The Dishonesty

The third part of an affair is dishonesty; the inevitable lying. An affair is always based on lying. If it weren't hidden, we wouldn't call it an affair. When you're found out, this can be the most difficult part for your marriage partner to forgive and overcome: the dishonesty; being lied to; and if you (most likely) denied the affair when first confronted, the double bind of not being trustworthy, even when you claim to be telling the truth.

Dishonesty in this context can mean anything from denying a full-fledged love affair with your spouse's best friend, for instance, to failing to mention an attraction to your tennis instructor.

Avoiding telling the truth and hoping your partner won't notice is a passive-aggressive form of dishonesty.

Billy and Leslie were in my office for couple's therapy, in recovery from Billy's affair. Billy had justified his affair by an implicit assumption that "What she doesn't know won't hurt her." Addressing me, Billy said, "Well, she never brought it up, she never asked."

He'd been cheating on Leslie for almost a year. His affair was particularly problematic for Leslie, she said, because Billy's affair partner was a man. And up until now, Leslie had had no idea that Billy had been interested in men.

"Billy, you never told me you were into guys," Leslie said in the therapy session.

Billy justified it. "It's totally for sex, it means nothing."

"That's not the point. You never told me you were cheating, I had to find out about it myself, you didn't tell me about it, and when I did find out, you denied it. Even up until we got to therapy, and then you insisted you were cheating with a woman."

"I'm not gay," he insisted.

"How do I know that?" she said. "You have lied about everything. So now I have no idea what's going on." Leslie had discovered Billy's cheating by finding a profile that he had created on a dating app. Billy had posted a naked photo of himself and advertised that he was looking to having sex with a man. When Leslie confronted him about his profile, he swore that someone must have stolen his identity and used his photo to post a fake profile on the site.

They had sought therapy to work through the crisis and he admitted in the first session that, yes, it was indeed his profile. He'd lied to her because he was embarrassed and didn't know how to tell her the truth.

More came out as the session progressed. Leslie had searched his email and found out that Billy had been meeting with one specific man on a regular basis. When she asked him about the relationship, he denied it.

With more time, and more therapy, Billy finally admitted that: "Yes, it's true, I've been seeing this one guy. But only one guy and only a few times."

But he was frustrated. He couldn't understand why Leslie wouldn't believe him that he was only interested in sex and that it wasn't gender-specific. He was quite clear with her that he was fluid in his sexuality, meaning he could have sex with "pretty much anyone, gay, bi, trans."

"I'm just 'into sex'," he insisted.

I explained to Billy that it wasn't just the sex that bothered Leslie and, according to her, it wasn't just the fact that the sex was with a man. What bothered Leslie was the fact that Billy continually lied to her.

"It's the dishonesty," she said. "If he had been forthright with me about the affair, if he hadn't denied it when I caught him, if he hadn't denied it all along, I might be able to trust him. But now whatever he tells me, everything he says, it's all tainted."

For Billy, telling the truth would have meant several things. He was frightened that Leslie wouldn't understand his desires. He had always felt he was more into sex than she was. And that she would never really "get him," that she would judge him if she knew what he was into. In order for him to be honest with her, he would have had to believe that she wouldn't belittle him or, worse, leave him.

If he'd trusted her, if he'd been honest with her in the first place, he would have had to share with Leslie his desire for 1) more sex, 2) a different kind of sex, and 3) sex with people other than her; and 4) he would have had to take a risk that she might reject him.

Many people act like Billy in the hope that they'll either never have to tell, or that they'll be able to explain about their affair and apologize if or when they do get caught.

The Different Kinds of Dishonesty

There's a difference between avoiding telling your partner something and outright lying to your partner when they confront you. Denying the truth when they look you in the eye is a different kind of dishonesty than when you think you're only protecting them from the truth by "casting shade" on an incident you'd rather forget.

If you're confronted, should you lie directly to them?

It's not a great strategy. Continuing to lie means you're avoiding the truth because you're afraid; afraid it will hurt them, afraid it will hurt you, afraid you'll lose something you have or never get that thing you want.

If you lie to your partner's face when they've confronted you, that's denial. If you lie to them because they suspect an affair, then you're trying to deny *their* reality. You may even be trying to convince them that their reality is crazy. This is called gaslighting.[1] To gaslight someone means to make them feel like their reality is a lie, even when they have proof.

Confrontation

Being confronted about your affair can be a shocking experience. You may feel ashamed that you haven't told the truth, particularly now that you've been caught. Face to face with the person you are hurting, the person with whom you are having an inside relationship, makes it all unpleasantly, startlingly real. The holiday's over; the vacation's ended—real life comes crashing down. You are totally snagged.

When you've been found out and are confronted with your cheating, you may have no choice but to admit that you have been lying. If you continue to deny, and lie, you'll only make it worse, for yourself and for your partner. But still, in that moment, you may still hedge;

---

[1] The term "gaslighting" comes from the 1944 film *Gaslight* with Ingrid Bergman and Charles Boyer. In the film, the newlywed character played by Bergman notices strange things going on in her house; pictures move, unexplained footsteps are heard, and the gaslights flicker on and off when no one else is in the house but her. She begins to imagine she's losing her mind, but it's her new husband who's ultimately responsible for tormenting her, in an attempt to drive her insane. "Gaslighting" someone means to sow seeds of doubt, and to undercut or confuse the truth.

you may be so agitated, so jolted by reality, that it feels like your world is collapsing.

And in some ways it is. The two worlds that you've compartmentalized are now smashing into one another. It's hard, maybe even impossible, to immediately decide what to do. Do you admit it? Come clean?

You've probably been thinking about this for a while, even if you have been in denial, putting it off, perhaps hoping this day would never come. You wondered if you would ever get caught. Maybe on some level you wanted it all to come out—it can be hard to keep a secret.

But you weren't prepared for this moment. Not yet. And so your lizard brain takes over.

Why People Lie

That ancient part of your brain, the lizard (or survival) brain—your brain stem—is the part of your brain that goes into fight, flight, or freeze response when you're in a crisis. Lying is a form of flight and deflecting may indicate you're in flight mode. Deflecting may sound something like, *"I have no idea what you are talking about. That's not my email. I don't even know anyone named blah-blah-blah!"*

Or you might respond by going into defensive fight mode. You could turn against your partner: *"Why are you looking at my emails? What do you think you're doing! This is an invasion of my privacy!"*

Or you could freeze. People who "freeze" in their lizard-brain response may find themselves literally incapable of doing or saying anything. If you respond this way under severe stress, during confrontation you may gape blankly at your partner as they demand answers. Your blank face could make them more agitated, which further shuts you down. You can't think. Your mind is empty. You want to disappear.

So, which are you? Flight, fight or freeze?

Do you naturally respond with the flight response: "I'm outta here." (Liars do this well.)

Or do you naturally respond with the fight response: "Why are you invading my privacy?" (Cheaters who argue are great at this.)

Or are you the freeze responder: "Huh? Are you talking to me?" (Conflict avoiders do this one perfectly.)

When you're in lizard-brain mode and feeling your fight, flight or freeze response, you can make another choice. There is a way to overcome your brain-stem reactivity.

Just come clean.

Integrity

Integrity means integrating all the parts of yourself. Can you really have an authentic relationship when there is a part of you that is compartmentalized and kept secret? If you feel like you aren't living with integrity, it doesn't matter what your partner thinks about you, it won't be easy to live with yourself. It may be time to come clean—for your own survival.

There's no guarantee your primary relationship will survive if you tell. However, there are some things you can do if you really want to make it work with your partner, or you just want to feel better about yourself. The following are some things to think about before you reveal all to your spouse.

Before you reveal your affair:

1) Is your affair really *over*?

2) If not, are you willing to *end it*?

3) Do you know *what you were looking for* in your affair?

4) Did you *learn* anything new about yourself from cheating?

5) Can you *let go* of the idea that your spouse is to blame?

6) Can you imagine a *new* kind of relationship with your spouse in the future?

7) Can you think about how *you* need to change?

Avoidance

If you "take flight" and leave the room, or try to turn the conversation to another matter, or deny, or minimize with comments like, *"We'll talk about this later; You're making much too much of this; It's nothing; I can't talk about this now, why are you making a scene? You are such a drama queen!"* this means you're minimizing or avoiding, which is another form of dishonesty. You might think that if you just avoid talking about it that you'll be off the hook. But avoiding conflict will only make things worse.

You may think that if you don't tell, that if you don't talk about the affair, then it's not a problem. "What they don't know won't hurt them."

Or you could dissemble.[1] Disguise what you really feel, avoid the truth. Make up some stuff.

But all of these responses will challenge not only

---

[2] **To dis·sem·ble də ˈsembəl/** verb
To conceal one's true motives, feelings, or beliefs.
An honest, sincere person has no need to dissemble.
Synonyms: dissimulate, pretend, feign, act, masquerade, sham, fake, bluff, posture, hide one's feelings, put on a false front
To disguise or conceal (a feeling or intention).

your relationship but your feelings about yourself. Can you live with the way you feel about yourself right now?

Doesn't Everybody Lie?

Maddie had cheated on Bo with four other men over the past few years. The "dalliances" were brief affairs that she'd managed to hide for some time, until the day she left her phone open. Bo had always assumed that Maddie's short business trips were so busy with deal-making that they didn't allow for anything else, including affairs, though he'd had his suspicions. But when he read her texts, Bo realized that all Maddie's infidelities had happened while she was traveling for work. Maddie was immediately dismissive and felt that her sex flings shouldn't matter to Bo. In fact, Bo had cheated on her, so what was the big deal?

"Honey, Bo, dear," she began in our session, "It's nothing. I don't know what you're so worried about."

"Um, the four guys you slept with?" Bo said.

"Oh, those. Just like your affairs, for sex only, right? No big deal. Everybody needs a little whatever, on the side. It's over, let's move on. These guys meant nothing to me. Nothing."

"You sent photos of yourself to each of these men. Naked photos."

"Okay, but you posted photos of yourself on that website. It's no big deal. Everyone does it these days."

I asked Maddie what she thought bothered Bo the most about her affairs. "I think he's angry because I am the woman and women don't cheat. But, whatever! It's fine, no big deal. We should just move on. It's over."

I wondered out loud to both of them why Maddie was minimizing her affairs. Was it because she was afraid of Bo's response? Was she afraid he would leave her? Was she exacting revenge for Bo's affairs? I asked her to think a little bit more about what she wanted from her marriage to Bo.

We'll get to more on Bo and Maddie, later.

Endnotes
vi   Brown, Emily 2013 Patterns of Infidelity and Their Treatment, Routledge, 2nd edition
vii Spring, Janis, After the Affair,

CHAPTER THREE
Tell or Don't,
But Don't Blame Your Spouse

Should you tell your partner about your affair? Maybe. Consider the options.

The Risks and Benefits

There are obvious risks in trying to keep an affair secret. There is a risk you may inadvertently blurt out the truth—a revelation that could harm your partner and your relationship permanently.

Your spouse may, eventually, uncover the affair and the extent of your lying—and the dishonesty may be deemed unforgiveable.

You also risk distancing yourself so much from your spouse that any hope of future reconciliation is impossible.

Keeping a secret like an affair means you live a double life, split off from your own integrity, never feeling truly yourself no matter who you are with or where you are.

Telling your partner could be positive for both of you. Coming clean with your infidelity could be the spark that "shakes up" a dormant marriage, leading both of you to make some much-needed changes.

Telling your partner may lead you both to take an honest look at where you are in your lives and what you want. This forces a crisis. Sometimes crisis, although painful, leads to major personal growth.

Confessing also relieves you of the burden of keeping such a heavy secret. But be careful—are you confessing to make yourself feel better despite whether this will hurt your partner?

Another Option?

Don't tell.

Telling your partner about an indiscretion might make you feel better. But are you unloading on them, only shaking up their secure world so that you can feel like you have a clear conscience?

Sometimes, if an affair is a mistake, telling your partner could mean the dissolution of your marriage, even though your infidelity was meaningless—something that barely mattered to you, but will have life-long consequences for your spouse and your family.

That doesn't mean you shouldn't tell.

Think about it clearly: Is it better to disclose the truth now, then if they were to discover it themselves later on?

If there's an issue in your marriage that's not improving, there may be a risk you'll cheat again if you don't address the issue now. Is now the time to confront what's going on with your marriage?

Or maybe this isn't about your marriage at all. Maybe you love your spouse and your infidelity has nothing at all to do with them. Your affair is *your* affair.

You might conceal your affair, or confront the truth directly, but don't blame your partner.

Ask Yourself
Here are some essential questions to ask yourself when you're considering coming clean.

1) What is to be gained by revealing the truth about my affair?

2) Will it make me feel better or will it make my partner feel better?

3) Am I ready to be transparent about who I am with my partner?

4) Would I want my partner to tell me the truth if

they were having an affair?

When You Are Confronted and Want to Tell the Truth

If your partner already suspects you of cheating and asks you directly, and you want to tell them the truth, there are things you can say to soften the blow, assuming you still want to stay together.

In Order for the Conversation to Go Smoothly:

1) Ask if this is a good time to **talk**.
2) Move somewhere **private** to have the conversation.
3) Don't lie to them if **they already know** the truth.
4) Tell the truth.
5) **Ask** specifically **what do they want to know**?
6) **Don't hide** anything.
7) Show **respect**.
8) Be **kind**.
9) Make eye contact: **hold** their hand.
10) **Show empathy,** but now is not the time to apologize

Trust

If you have this conversation, know that your spouse may not trust you for a long time, if ever again. Still, commit to telling them the truth. Their trust issues aren't just about you. They'll need to learn to trust themselves again, to trust their own intuition, and they'll be angry; angry at you, but also angry at themselves for not trusting their gut or for not seeing what was right in front of them.

Maybe they suspected, but they told themselves not to believe their own truth, or maybe they knew but didn't want to know. The anger of the cheated-on spouse is real, and you can't wish it away or apologize and hope it calms down.

If you cheated because the truth is you wanted to get out of the marriage, admit to it—to yourself and to your spouse. Don't make them break up with you. Having an affair can be a passive-aggressive way of forcing your spouse to end your marriage. If you think that's why you did it, be honest.

Need for Validation

It's easy to justify your cheating behavior, particularly if you feel entitled to your outside relationship. You may be at a time in your life in which you feel the need for attention and validation—something you're not getting at home. But don't lay blame for that on your spouse. If you truly feel that you "deserved" an affair, keep that to yourself. Instead, go to therapy and talk to someone neutral, to work through your resentment and your entitlement. Then have the talk with your spouse where you reveal your affair.

How to Tell Your Spouse

If you do choose to disclose the affair to your spouse before you are confronted, here's an exercise that may help you prepare.

Use the following worksheet to help guide you when revealing the affair to your spouse. You'll want to handle this conversation with respect, dignity and compassion. Remember, what you're about to reveal to your spouse will undoubtedly hurt; you'll need to show empathy and kindness.

And think about these five things below before you begin. If you don't agree with these, you may not be ready to tell your partner.

One. You're about to reveal something that will cause pain; nothing your spouse has done to you, up to this point, matters. Don't make this conversation about revenge for things they've done to you in the past. This conversation is purely to disclose your affair. This isn't the time to tell your spouse how you feel about them, or about your marriage. Do not do any finger-pointing.

Two. Your spouse is not an extension of you. They'll make up a story about what this affair means to them that has nothing to do with you. Allow them their own reality. Don't tell them what they should be feeling; allow them to express their feelings. Don't let the words "you are wrong" come out of your mouth. (For how to deal with disagreement, keep reading.)

Three. Keep this conversation focused on the basic information about the affair. You don't have to tell your spouse specific details about when, where, how many times, or even with whom you had the affair. That may come, in time, if you decide it's best for them to know details.

Four. Make an appointment to talk to your spouse. Let them know you have something important to discuss. Make sure they're available and open to discussion. You don't have to tell them what you are going to share, but let them know you'll need at least an hour of their time. After your disclosure, remind your spouse that this is not the end of the conversation. Tell them when you can talk next.

Five. Honor the "why" questions your spouse will have. (See the following for more on this.)

The First Conversation

Ask for an Appointment.

One. **Make an Appointment**: Ask your spouse, "Is now a good time to sit down and talk? I have something to talk with you about and we are going to need <u>some time/an hour/a couple of hours/some privacy</u>." *[If now is not a good time, ask for a meeting at a time that is more comfortable for them. Avoid alcohol and drugs, and be in a weapon-free environment.]*[2]

Two. **Warn Them**: "I have something to talk about that is very difficult, and I know what I'm about to say will be painful. I'm <u>nervous/scared/ emotional</u>." *[Choose what you feel and be honest].*

Three. **Tell Them**: "I have been having an affair." *[Be direct. Do not avoid the conflict.]* **Or:** "I *had* an affair." **Or:** "I have been having an affair since ____ ." *[It's your choice which and how many details to reveal. Consider the consequences of what you reveal and why. Give as much information as you can.]*

---

2 *Most domestic violence occurs between men and women when a woman tries to leave a tense situation. If you feel that your conversation could escalate quickly—if there is abuse in your home—get help and avoid any conversations with your spouse that could lead to violence.*

Four. <u>Stay or Go</u>: "I want to stay in our marriage." **Or**: "I want to leave our marriage." *[Tell your spouse your immediate thoughts about your goals.]*

Five. <u>**What Do You Want?**</u> "I want to stay in the affair." "I want to end the affair." "I am ambivalent about the affair." *[Tell your spouse your immediate thoughts about your affair. Acknowledge that these thoughts can change at any time. Try not to lie.]*

Six. <u>**Vision**</u>: Tell your spouse what you hope will happen with your marriage: "I want to start anew, I hope to go to couple's therapy and/or individual therapy." *[Acknowledge you have no control over your spouse's decisions.]*

Seven. <u>**Be Clear About What You Need**</u>: "I need you to not tell the children for now." "I need to cancel our vacation." "I need to go to rehab." "I need a separation." *[It doesn't mean you will get what you need but you have more of a chance if you state your needs clearly.]*

Eight. <u>**Empathize**</u>: "I can only imagine what you must be feeling. I imagine you are angry/hurt/have questions. I want to hear everything you want to say." *[Listen to what they have to say.]*

Nine. **Ask What They Want in This Moment**: "Do you want to talk more now or should we talk later?" *[If you are overwhelmed and can't listen to more at this moment, tell them that you can't take in any more information at this time, and that you're having a hard time listening so you need to take a time out.]*

Ten. **Ask What They Want for the Immediate Future:** "Do you want me to sleep in another room? Move out of the bedroom? Leave the house for the night?" *[Tell them what you need in the immediate future if it differs from what they need.]*

Eleven. **Tell Them Only What You Are Willing to Tell:** "It makes sense you want all those details. I can't talk about that now." **Or:** "I can tell you who/when/how many times." *[Decide what you will reveal now and what you will reveal later, or in therapy, and what is off limits for now.]*

Twelve. **Be direct if this is over:** "I want to end our marriage." **Or:** "I think this is a sign that our marriage is complete." **Or:** "I think our marriage should end." **Or:** "I think you and I are over, and we should end things now."*[This may not be the time to say the word "divorce"* *which can be "activating." You are already using the word "affair," which is emotional and will trigger a crisis. Wait and have a separate talk about divorce at another time.]*

Now That You've Confessed

You've revealed your affair to your spouse and they've reacted with surprise. You might be surprised by their surprise. You might think there's no way they couldn't have known all this time. How could they not have suspected? After all, you left so many hints and clues along the way. But still, they registered shock.

Sometimes spouses suppress the truth to themselves to such an extent that they are in deep denial. They may have suspected, but finding out the truth can still be a terrible blow. Give them the respect they are due and acknowledge that, yes, this is a life-changing revelation and things may never be the same.

Now They Want Details

It's almost certain your partner will want more details—curiosity is natural. Sharing too many details of the affair won't benefit you or your partner right now. My advice is to keep your conversation to **three key areas** of the affair:

1) What kind of relationship you had. (Was it sexual or emotional?)
2) What kind of sex you had. (Was it casual, online, paid?)
3) And what secrets you kept. (Did you spend money? Did you tell others?)

Trying to make sense of the affair, to understand its depth, they may want to know how many times you slept together, whether the sex was better or different than what you shared, where you had sex, how much larger their breasts are/or how much longer their penis is, how they measured up in other ways, how many times you texted, called, said "I love you," whispered in their ear, talked in person, ate dinner, breakfast, lunch, had coffee, or kissed.

But if you answer all of these questions, your partner may not ever be able to forget the details of what happened, when instead they are looking for reassurance, comfort and a sign that your affair is over. Be clear with them that you want to be honest, but you also know that details may not be helpful.

Ask them:

What are you really longing for when you ask that question?

What can I say to you to answer your real question?

Is there another question underneath that question?

How Many Questions Should You Answer?

The risk for you is that you could end up using your partner as your confessor. You might make the mistake of telling your spouse too many details, just to get the questions over with—and the affair over with. You might fall into another trap when your partner says, "Just tell me everything, if you tell me all the details, everything, then I'll feel better/forgive you/forget."

Don't share the details of the affair trying to find absolution, to let go of your own shame and guilt, to confess to someone the story you've been holding onto, to let go of the burden you've been keeping. Your spouse may be your best friend, someone you've been intimate with, maybe even for a long while. It might feel good to confess to the person with whom you normally share your most intimate thoughts.

But your partner is not your priest or your therapist. You shouldn't unburden the details of your affair onto your spouse. It might alleviate your guilt, but it could traumatize them.

Detective Mode

Your spouse, on the other hand, might be in detective

mode and grill you for details to try and extract all your closely guarded secrets. Therapists, in the past, have encouraged this type of confession, advising couples that it was best if the cheater gave in to all requests for details from the non-cheating spouse. These well-meaning therapists would even suggest that the cheater answer any question that the spouse asked, no matter how intimate or revealing. The theory behind this approach was that only when all the cheated-upon spouse's curiosity had run out, could the healing begin. You can probably guess how well that worked!

Curiosity is a bottomless pit. The non-cheating spouse will never run out of questions if given free rein. And it will be exhausting for both of you. The endless digging, exploring, spelunking and diving will always lead to more questions for the cheater. "Where did you go last August and what did you have for lunch and when was the first time you did this and where did you do that and…."

The Narrative of the Affair

A more effective and healing approach is to discuss the narrative underneath the affair. A narrative means talking about what the infidelity means to you, the cheater, and for your partner to take a look at the story of the affair and what it means for them. And then for both of you to discuss what this affair means to each of you and to your relationship, both past, and future.

For instance, if your partner continues to push for details about the affair, you may instead encourage them to explore:

1) What do you think my affair says about me?
2) What do you think my affair says about you?
3) What do you think my affair says about us?

This is a much more valuable conversation, for you and your partner, (and your affair partner as well). The answers to these questions reveal the meaning behind the affair. What the relationship means to you, and what you believe it means to others involved in it, will change over time, but it's important to take a look at these narratives to understand why you cheated, and why you think you chose your cheating partner in the first place.

It helps to write out the answers to these questions so you can take a serious look at the stories you make up about the infidelity and what they mean to you and to your life. Share this narrative with a therapist or keep it in a journal. Or use it as a basis for conversation with your spouse if you choose to have a deeper conversation about the affair. No matter what you do, it will be valuable to revisit this narrative over time to understand what it says about you.

CHAPTER FOUR
Stop Saying I'm Sorry

Most people who cheat are sorry they hurt their spouse. But they don't regret the affair. They don't regret cheating. They regret that they got caught. They regret that other people got caught up in the web of lies, or that they wasted so much of their lives hiding, or that the press found out, or that they were exposed on the internet, or that they were followed by a detective and someone took photos of them, or that their kids or their constituents or their parish found out. But they don't regret their affair and they aren't sorry for cheating.

Most people enjoy cheating. They revel in their affairs. They have fun. They have intense feelings of belonging and desire, and they have exciting sexual encounters.

Regret?

According to Ashley Madison[3], 47 percent of cheaters

---

3   Survey of 1,369 members of Ashley Madison between July 19, 2018 - July 29, 2018

who registered as members on the company's website said they wouldn't do anything differently about their affairs, while 93 percent said they're very happy with the outcome of their infidelity.

This doesn't mean you aren't sorry for hurting your loved ones. But if you are the type of cheater that doesn't regret anything except the hurt, don't pretend that you regret the affair.

If you have been caught or disclosed your affair, stop saying "I'm sorry" over and over again—if it's meaning-less. If you don't regret the outside relationship, those words barely penetrate the surface when you apologize.

Empathy

How many times have you said it? Until you really know what you are apologizing for, it helps to change your strategy.

The goal here is not to say "I'm sorry," but to find **empathy** for what your partner is going through.

Evan and Anna came to my office after Evan's affair. Anna was devastated by Evan's long-term infidelity with a co-worker, someone he'd been seeing for more than two years. Complicating matters, he'd developed feelings for the much younger woman and had helped pay for her college degree while he continued to see her to have sex. Angered when she discovered the ongoing affair, Anna demanded he stop seeing the coworker. Anna not only felt sexually betrayed by Evan, she felt financially betrayed, as well.

"Evan has probably said 'I'm sorry' to me, like, one hundred times, and every time he says it, it means less. Each time he says it, I feel like he is just trying to placate me." Anna cried in the couple's therapy session.

"I always thought actions meant more than words anyway," Evan said. But he kept saying he was sorry because he thought Anna needed to hear it, and he had no idea what else to do to make it up to her.

"Actions don't mean more than words in this case," I explained. "You can do lots of great things, but it doesn't change what you did, right Evan?"

"Yes," Anna responded, "and your 'I'm sorry' still means nothing. How will I ever trust you again?"

Evan was truly sorry, but not for the affair. He was sorry for hurting Anna, his wife. I asked him: "If Anna didn't mind, or if she didn't know, would you continue to see this girl?"

He looked around the office, shyly. The hair around his bald spot gleamed in the soft afternoon light of my office. "I guess, if it really didn't hurt her, if she didn't know, I would. The girl, well, she helped me a lot, with the, you know, she made me feel stuff. I know she was a lot younger than me, but she helped with the erectile issues, she helped, you know?"

Anna almost jumped off the couch as if to physically confront Evan. I stopped her.

"Anna, does it make sense that Evan isn't sorry for the affair because it helped him and, in a way, it helped you. Until you hear what he has to say, I don't think you understand what it meant to Evan. How can either of you actually have empathy for each other's feelings if you don't really talk about it and try to understand? Let's focus on what you feel in the present moment about what happened."

I asked Evan to share with Anna the story he made up about what the affair meant to him and about Anna, and about their relationship. "Remember," I said, "*the story we make up* is our own take on reality and is going to be different than our partners. To Evan, the affair meant "that I was not really a cheater because I never would have left Anna for this girl; she wasn't the marrying kind, not for me."

I stopped him. "So, you had an implicit monogamy assumption that this wasn't really a threat to your marriage?"

"Well, not for me, but I know Anna won't agree."

"So, the story you made up about what this meant about Anna…"

"I made up that the affair was a way to save my pride. Because Anna would think less of me if she knew I had such bad erectile dysfunction. She doesn't have much patience with such things. And where we are from, we don't talk much about personal stuff like that."

Anna looked at him sharply.

"Go on," I said.

"And what it meant about us, or what I made up that it meant about us, was that it was helping us. I learned how to work with my personal, you know, erection issues, and it wasn't taking away from our marriage."

"Anna, does it make sense that he felt that way?" The idea was to get Anna and Evan to empathize with each other's feelings, which is more important than an apology, or an agreement. If they could understand what it's like to be in each other's shoes, then they could validate each other's experience, which meant they could find some peace in the situation.

"I don't get it," Anna said.

"Well," I said, "in reality, without the pressure of being in a committed relationship with this woman, Evan sounds like he was able to get around his erectile dysfunction. Does it make sense that he would feel that she was helping him and, by extension, helping you, and your marriage?"

Anna replied with, "Well, what I make up about what the affair meant to me is that Evan was no longer attracted to me and that he apologizes all the time just to appease me, so that he can keep going to her, and that what it means about him is that he is probably in love with her. I mean, he is paying for her college education, for goodness sake! And what it means about us is that we are going to stay together and be miserable—like my parents." Her face turned red and she sat stonily on the couch with her arms crossed.

Evan looked across at her in shock. "Anna, I am not in love with her. I'm embarrassed. I was always embarrassed to talk to you about my erectile dysfunction. And so that's all it was. And I felt like I owed her, because she helped me, that's all. And she is, yes, a nice girl."

"Evan, I'm not upset about your sexual dysfunction. So what if you can't get an erection? That's not why I love you. And I actually don't care that you paid for her college, honestly—I think it's sweet, and that's why I love you because you are so damn generous."

He looked at her and smiled, and they hugged.

There was more work to be done, and more therapy

to be had, but the answer was not a simple "I'm sorry." The goal is to find a place of empathy, where each partner can understand the other's inner experience and try to empathize with each other's story.

What They Really Want to Know

If you want to be honest when confronted by your partner, and not just mumble the standard "I'm sorry" (and if you want to stay out of your lizard brain), it helps to:

1) Not blame
2) Not deny
3) Not dissemble
4) Think clearly about what you want to tell about your cheating.

What your partner really wants to know is: why?

The Number One Question Your Partner Has: Why? Why did you cheat?

Your spouse will ask you a lot of other questions, like: where, when, how, who—as well as specific inquiries in their search for more details of your affair. But their primary concern—the question underlying all these other questions—is why? *Why* did you cheat on me?

It's hard to answer the "why" question without blaming or dissembling or re-evaluating your whole relationship.

What to Say

You don't have to rewrite the history of your marriage in order to answer this question with honesty and integrity. You don't have to go through the chronicle of your childhood, and you don't have to justify the affair by detailing all the positive qualities of your affair partner(s).

You most definitely do *not* want to list all the physical attributes of your affair partner, or describe how beautiful or handsome or successful they are, or how great the sex is/was. You want to try to avoid comparing your affair partner and your spouse; that's definitely something you should never do.

Whether or not you believe you're trading up with your affair partner, you still have a relationship with the person in front of you. Figure out what happened, first, before you jump ship, even if that's your ultimate intent.

When your spouse or committed partner asks you "*Why?*" several reasons may immediately come to mind: *you were lonely, you were in love, you were angry at your spouse, you don't believe in monogamy, it just happened, it was a mistake, it only happened one time, you are no longer attracted to your spouse, you are in a sexless marriage, you met someone you had chemistry with, you went on a dating site out of curiosity, it was exciting, the sex was amazing, you want a divorce but you are staying for the kids and this is the next best thing.*

If just one, or if all, of the above reasons are true, you should consider deeply before answering the "Why" question your partner is putting in front of you.

The Can Opener Affair

Sometimes an affair is what I call a "can opener," or a way to get out of a marriage. You may not have the voice (or courage) to say you want out, so you cheat. You may not realize you want out of your marriage until you cheat, and then you realize your marriage is over. Or you may be forcing your partner to break up with you by cheating on them and unconsciously (or not) hoping to be found out. It can be a passive-aggressive way of ending your marriage, a way of avoiding conflict and not taking responsibility for directly ending your relationship. A "can opener affair" typically destroys the marriage when your partner finds out (and ultimately, they will, because you'll make sure they do).

What Made Me Do It?

Instead of apologizing, with no real meaning behind your "I'm sorry," let's get to the truth behind what you're saying, and understand why you're doing it. This way if you want to have an authentic conversation with your partner, you will be able to provide some insight into what made you do it.

Once you understand what kind of affair you're having, it will be easier to decide: 1) If you should end your affair; or 2) If you should end your marriage. Treat these as separate and distinct decisions. Understand this before you try to explain the affair or your motivations.

The Wake-Up or Break-Up Affair

Most affairs are what I call "wake-up or break-up" relationships. Some are specifically a wake-up call, in the hope that your partner will pay attention to you or your needs. These affairs are can also be a wake-up call to you, the cheater—to force you to ask yourself, "What the heck am I doing?"

Jenna had been cheating for a few months. She was married and had a boyfriend with whom she met every few days, purely for sex. But she wasn't happy. Her two boys were in middle school and needed constant shuttling around from sports to school events. Jenna and the kids would arrive home late in the evening and she would make dinner, help with homework and get them ready for bed. Her husband Noah worked late and at the end of the day spent his evenings slumped in front of the television.

Noah rarely initiated sex and when Jenna tried Noah went along grudgingly.

Jenna lay awake at night, unable to sleep. She was slowly realizing that sex was never going to be as satisfying as it was in their first years of marriage when they had no children and fewer responsibilities.

Jenna had begun an affair with Mike, against her better judgment, and she was shocked at her own behavior. The affair had been going on for four months when she entered therapy. Jenna told me in her individual session, "The sex with Mike is amazing. I have multiple orgasms every time. And it feels great to be wanted all the time. But now Mike is asking me to leave my husband. He wants to be with me, like move in with me. It scares me. Really scares me. He even sort of low-level threatened me. He said he would call Noah, my husband, and tell him everything. If I wouldn't tell Noah, Mike said he would."

Jenna still loved her husband Noah and she had kids and responsibilities. She liked Mike; he was great, and the sex was truly amazing. But this whole experience—this affair—was really a wake-up call. She found she didn't want to start another serious relationship with a different man. She didn't want to work at trying to make a new long-term partnership work. The affair had been a way to get the sex she wanted. But if she was going to invest emotionally she would try and renew her relationship with her husband.

"What the hell am I doing?" she asked herself. She hoped Noah would never find out. "No, the sex with Noah isn't great," she said. "And, yes, I will always remember Mike for the good times, but it has to end."

Jenna was really struggling. Should she talk to Noah? Try to get him into therapy? Would things ever change? She wondered about her friends and acquaintances. How were their marriages?

Jenna's not the only wife and mother having an affair. According to available data, there are almost as many wives who cheat as there are cheating husbands.

On Ashley Madison,[4] there are actually more women using the site than men.[5] For every one active paid male there are 1.13 active females as verified in a recent Ernst and Young report[6].

Ashley Madison[7] recently surveyed its members and

---

4   Based on the number of members who have joined since 2002.

5   It is important to note that men pay to use the site, while women use the site for free.

6   https://www.ashleymadison.com/2017report

7   Survey of 2,767 members of Ashley Madison between June 19, 2018, and July 5, 2018.

found that sixty-seven percent of the female respondents have more and better sex after they join the site. It seems that married women who cheat have better sex with their partners when they are having affairs.

Why Are You Different Outside of Your Marriage?

It can be tempting to stray outside of your marriage, to explore more passion and to try to find the excitement you might be missing. Maybe you feel you can only be your most passionate self outside of your marriage. You may want to think about why this is. Our own sexual personalities change and instead of growing closer, we grow more distant from our partners (even affair partners).

Sex, after the initial romantic phase of a relationship, can become less frequent and more routine over time. The emotional connection dissipates and many people look for excitement outside the marriage. This may be because you can be different parts of your personality with each new person you meet. In each new relationship, you become a new person. A new affair can bring out a part of you that you may not be able to show your spouse.

You will exhibit different parts of your personality depending on whether you're with your spouse, or with your extramarital partner. Forty-two percent of male and female respondents of the same Ashley Madison survey say that when they're in bed with their spouse, they're more reserved and tend to describe the sex as more traditional. However, with their affair partner they are much more adventurous. Fifty-three percent describe themselves as more playful with their affair partner while 40 percent say they are totally wild in bed.[viii]

Living in Two Different Worlds

There are many reasons why a couple can grow apart sexually. Finding someone outside the marriage can sometimes be easier than trying to improve the sex life you have with your current partner. "When asked, eight-five percent of Ashley Madison survey respondents say that they have to initiate sex with their spouse, whereas fifty-five percent of females say that that their affair partner initiates sex most often.[8]

The following are the results of an Ashley Madison survey with cheating respondents:[ix]

---

8   Survey of 2,767 members of Ashley Madison between June 19, 2018, and July 5, 2018.

<u>Females describe their sexual personality as:</u>

I'm always horny/in the mood—48 percent

I'm curious/like to try new things—44 percent

I like to be dominated—37 percent

<u>Males describe their sexual personality as:</u>

I'm always horny/in the mood—62%

I'm curious/ like to try new things—42%

I like to be dominated—28%

Changing it up

Respondents had an adventurous sexual side, but this sexual adventurousness mostly came out with their extramarital partners, rather than with their spouses. With a spouse, just over 30 percent of females say their favorite sex position is missionary, but with their affair partner, they prefer doggy-style (41 percent) and cowgirl—when the woman is on top but facing her partner (29 percent).

The male respondents preferred the cowgirl position with both their spouse and their affair partner, with 52 percent also preferring to role-play, as well.

In the end, whether it's role-playing or changing up the positions, 81 percent reported they like to try new things sexually—but most often with their affair partners rather than with their spouses.

So is This a Wake-Up Call?

If this is a "wake-up call" affair it can trigger the awakening of a dormant, or stagnant, part of your personality, which can lead to renewal of some part of you that has the capacity for more passion and more pleasure.

You'll know because the passionate part of you won't just be "awake" with your affair partner. You'll feel sexier with yourself; you might find you masturbate more, you desire sexier clothes, you feel younger, you start working out, you get a better haircut. You'll feel better in your clothes, you'll feel more erotic in your fantasy life. This doesn't happen just because you met someone new. It happens because you *are* someone new.

The question is, can you be this new self with your current partner? Can you integrate this new part of yourself into a new life, without blaming anyone but yourself for feeling cut off and unaware of this up until now newly discovered part of you?

Sometimes an affair can create the opportunity for a self-discovery. To wake up, to remember a part of the self they miss, or that they long for, in themselves. It's nice to find the younger self, the sexier self, the part that you want to be.

Blowing Things Up

It can also trigger a much-needed dialogue between you

and your marriage partner. Sometimes a spouse cheats as an unconscious way to disrupt the current relationship but *not* to totally blow it apart. In these instances, the affair becomes a tool to force change in a marriage, not to end it.

If your marriage or long-term relationship is no longer satisfying and stuck at an impasse, and you've "fallen into" an affair, the knowledge of your infidelity may be the only thing to jolt you and your spouse or partner into awareness. Faced with a rude awakening, your spouse may begin taking you more seriously, leading to conversations about what you both want, and what you are willing to do to get it.

Your partner will most likely feel hurt by your cheating, and that may be *exactly* what you intended: for them to feel hurt as much as you've been hurting. You're forcing your spouse to realize that your needs are being ignored and that, although you've been mostly happy with your relationship, you crave a stronger sexual connection, or more intimacy, or something else. But did you want to hurt your partner to get the sexual attention you have been craving?

Maybe it was really YOU that you were craving? Give this some thought.

Either way, your act of infidelity has made it clear that if your relationship remains stagnant, you'll find sex and intimacy elsewhere.

Endnotes

viii   Ashley Madison (AshleyMadison.com) data reveals that women have more sex after joining– (July 7, 2018) - Ashley Madison, the world's leading married dating website, surveyed its members to find out if their sexual personality traits differ between partners, and what kinds of sexual behavior they bring into the bedroom - Survey of 2,767 members of Ashley Madison between June 19, 2018, and July 5, 2018.

ix   SURVEY reference

CHAPTER FIVE
Sometimes It's Just Chemistry

If you can heal and move forward, the affair will truly be a wake-up call. You may develop a renewed empathy for your yourself, and this could be the cornerstone of a more mature, more enduring partnership.

A crisis of infidelity in a marriage brings to the surface inadequacies within your relationship. Dealing effectively with this kind of a crisis could mark the beginning of a new kind of ongoing and improved communication. This could spark the kind of change needed to have a new kind of marriage. It may bring out some of the more healthier and loving aspects of both of you.

However, an affair can also reveal all of the previously contained and ignored anger or ill-will or neglect that's eroded your marriage. A "can opener" affair could be a step toward breaking up your unhealthy, unhappy partnership. When thinking about your affair, ask yourself: "Am I trying to wake up or break up my marriage?"

Sometimes it's Just Chemistry

Laurie met Dawn at a time when her marriage to Stella was cooling off, to the point of being "ice cold," she said.

"Stella and I haven't had sex in a long—I mean, *a long*—time. And I was always initiating it when we did have it. I mean, our relationship was cozy, I was happy, but then I met Dawn. It was totally hot—what a rush!"

For Stella and Laurie, their long-term relationship was nice and it was comforting, and they were good companions—an important part of any relationship. A marriage, or any committed partnership, is made up of two parts: *companionship* and *eroticism.* The companionship or day-to-day aspect of the relationship is the "roommate" part of your relationship. In Stella and Laurie's case, it worked well: they liked to watch TV and walk the dog, and they loved traveling together. But the other and equally important part of marriage is eroticism. A healthy and robust eroticism in a relationship makes for a passionate and *in-love* couple—for Stella and Laurie, this half of their relationship was an area in which they had assumed that being good roommates would lead to an erotic connection.

But like many couples, working on the erotic part needs to be a priority or it will fall to the bottom of the list. The neglect of their erotic life can mean that a couple relies solely on companionship, accepting that they might be better roommates, while still hoping that the sexual aspect of their partnership will somehow fix itself. When it doesn't, one or both eventually grow dissatisfied.

Many long-term couples come to me for therapy complain that they "love their partner" but that they're no longer "in love." Stella and Laurie still loved each other and they were good companions. But the passion, the erotic aspect of their relationship, had dissolved and neither knew how to get it back.

When Laurie met Dawn, she realized how much a part of her missed the passion. With Dawn, she felt like she'd woken up; and she liked the sexual attention. She wanted to be physically desired, and it felt good to be in lust with another woman.

Cheating with Dawn led to intense and mixed emotions: she hated lying to her wife Stella, but the cheating was thrilling and sexy. Surreptitiously making contact, meeting Dawn for secret assignations, finding clandestine places for sharing a meal—it was all exciting. And for good reason: having an affair releases brain chemicals that create a rush of intensity, which makes for an invigorating relationship.

Sneaking around increases the adrenaline that is released in what we normally think of as a "rush," helping our body to react quickly when it needs to, increasing our heart rate and increasing blood flow to our brain and muscles. Dopamine, the pleasure hormone, is responsible for that "dopey" feeling that enables us to feel good when we're doing things that are "bad." The fear of being caught releases endorphins into our body which also leaves us with feelings of well-being.

During their affair, Laurie and Dawn liked to rendezvous outside, taking long walks together in the woods or on the beach, where they had what Laurie called "long make-out sessions." This isn't uncommon in affairs: many people who cheat are forced to meet in secluded areas to avoid detection, and these locations, surrounded as they are by nature, can add an element of romance. Beauty in nature reduces stress hormones and boosts serotonin, as well, which decreases depression and creates a feeling of relaxation.

Sex can also produce serotonin, eliciting a nice, warm afterglow. Post-orgasm, both partners experience a flush of oxytocin—this "cuddle hormone" can bring a sense of tranquility and even trigger a sense of being in love.[x]

Laurie and Dawn's affair lasted almost two years. Eventually the brain-chemical effect wore off, as it does for most people after the initial excitement of a relationship dims. Laurie went back to Stella and told her about her affair. They decided to stay together and tried to make their marriage more exciting. Laurie took Stella for walks in the woods and on the beach but found it only reminded her of her relationship with Dawn. As of the writing of this book, Laurie and Stella are still working to repair their marriage.

Who is More Likely to Cheat?

Studies[xi] show that people with a certain variant of the dopamine D4 receptor gene are more likely to cheat on their partner. (The variant-D4-gene people are often re-ferred to by researchers as dopamine junkies, though the term isn't scientific and is considered pejorative.) Those with the variant gene are more likely to take risks and may even enjoy putting themselves in dangerous circum-stances. They're able to tolerate high-stress situations; more so than most people, who prefer to avoid stressful, high-risk environments.

According to some studies[xii] the hormone vasopres-sin is higher in people who tend toward monogamy. In studies with prairie voles and mountain voles, the moun-tain voles were found to have significantly lower levels of vasopressin than their more monogamous prairie vole[9] cousins. Vasopressin levels appear to affect bonding and mate choices. These studies also indicate that humans with higher levels of vasopressin would be more monogamous than those with lower levels.

It may be that for some couples, the affair relationship is hormonally driven. Cheating ratchets up the hormones released in the pleasure centers of the brain. Laurie described her affair with Dawn as purely chemical, it felt different. It wasn't at all like the committed relationship she had with Stella; one in which the chemical romance had more or less dissipated.

"With Dawn, well, every time I was around her it was like something went off in my brain and I couldn't control it. When Dawn and I touched, it was magic. I couldn't *stop* touching her. And the sex was, well, it was fabulous. After sex, we would lie around holding each other for hours. But, the funny thing is, if I didn't see her for a couple of days I didn't even think about her. It was like it never happened. I think it was easier to give her up after we stopped meeting in person. We spoke by phone for a while, but it wasn't the same. If I saw her, it would

---

9   https://www.nature.com/news/gene-switches-make-prairie-voles-fall-in-love-1.13112

have started all over again. It was the smell of her, the touch of her skin, her taste—I couldn't get past it."

Affairs of Opportunity

Brain chemicals aside, most affairs happen because of opportunity.

The *opportunity* to cheat can be a stronger motivator than any other reason to cheat. It's very hard to deny the temptation to cheat when it's right in front of you. If the possibility of an affair becomes intriguing enough to by-pass your normal reticence, and at the same time if your needs aren't being met at home, cheating may be too hard to resist.

Things could be going well with your spouse, but if you meet someone who is attracted to you; someone who challenges and flatters you and who, in addition, convinces you that this is an opportunity to find a part of yourself that is lost or denied in yourself, you may cross a line into an affair.

Referring to research, cultural critic Wednesday Martin writes[xiii], "There's now a pretty broad consensus among anthropologists that we evolved as cooperative breeders and, in our evolutionary prehistory, we likely did not live in monogamous [pairings]… we lived in loose, rangy bands of people, raising our offspring cooperatively and mating to multiply."[xiv]

So maybe you didn't seek it out, maybe "it just happened." If that's the case, you aren't alone: 35 to 55 percent of people having affairs report they were happy in their marriage at the time of the infidelity.[xv] Many also admit to still enjoying marital sex, even while having affairs.[xvi]

The affairs are often a place to bring the part of the self that is fun, more fun perhaps than the married part of the self.

In her book, *The State of Affairs*,[xvii] Esther Perel wrote: "I often say to my patients that if they could bring into their marriage even one-tenth of the boldness, the playfulness, and the verve that they bring to their affair, their home life would feel quite different. Our creative imagination seems to be richer when it comes to our transgressions than to our commitments."

If the opportunity for an extramarital affair presented itself, think about how this opportunity came to be. Did you purposely put yourself in this path of possibility? Were you seeking out more stimulating company or situations? Were you craving more intimacy and looking to connect with new people?

It doesn't matter so much that the person you're cheating with isn't the sort of person—or even the gender—you thought you'd be with, or the one you imagined you'd choose. It's a fact that sometimes men cheat with men, even if they identify as heterosexual. And women sometimes cheat with women, even though they identify as straight. Lisa Diamond, who authored *Sexual Fluidity*,[xviii] believes that women in particular become attracted to the person rather than the gender. She writes that, "... for women on average, desire often emerges from emotional closeness ... and can frequently ... impel heterosexual women into lesbian relationships ... it can redirect erotic attraction." One reason for this phenomenon, she suggests, may be found in what we discussed earlier, the hormone and chemical response. When oxytocin - the neurotransmitter unique to mammalian brains - is released, it can facilitate feelings of trust and well-being, and in female prairie voles [remember the monogamous species of rodent?], it can connect the act of sex to the formation of faithful attachments."

It may be that who we hang out with most are the people we have the most opportunity to be attracted to. And it is in these "rangy bands" of people where we might find our affairs.

Women and Affairs

According to most online dating websites that cater to married members, women are looking for affair partners just as often as men. Perel writes that, since the 1990s, the rate of married woman who cheat has increased by 40 percent. The rate among men, however, has remained the same. Although this behavior isn't new, what is new is the technology that facilitates "an equal opportunity playing field" for cheaters.

A century ago, even fifty years ago, women cheated with the milkman or the postman. The joke was that if little Timmy's hair was red, and Dad and Mom each had brown hair, then maybe the milkman was a redhead. Since most women's lives were circumscribed, usually bounded by home, the neighborhood and the marketplace, their daily contact with potential affair partners was usually limited to delivery men, salesmen, or the neighbor's husband.

Today, with unlimited autonomy and mobility, women have as many opportunities as men to cheat. They're in the workplace, they travel for work, and they meet people from all walks of life in all manner of places. Modern society has enabled equal opportunities for infidelity and cheating while married, which is now balanced between the sexes.

To state that men have a higher "sex drive" than women and are therefore driven to cheat more often simply isn't true. *Martin writes,* "We have inherited this cultural script... and been taught that men are more naturally sexual, that they have stronger libidos, that monogamy is harder for men, and men crave novelty and variety of sexual experience more than women do. We have been taught that this is 'science.' And what I learned when I talked to experts is that this very pat narrative began to fall apart."

Martin reports that the flawed assumption that men want to cheat more than women is based on an outdated study that assessed the mating patterns of male and female fruit flies, not people. And on additional science, recently debunked, that asserted females didn't benefit from mating multiply. In many species, we now know, they clearly do.

A more recent study, from January 2018, reveals that more women than men—between the ages of 18 and 29—had cheated. In a recent interview Martin said, "According to several national surveys, there's no really big, statistically significant infidelity gap until men and women hit their fifties."

Martin's review of anthropological data and interviews with anthropologists have led her to consider that, "In certain, far from rare ecological circumstances, it was and still is beneficial for women to be "promiscuous" because it conferred benefits. for example, a wider variety of sperm allows a female to hedge against male infertility, and up the odds of heterozygosity--a good genetic match. it might also be a great strategy to get more men to think the offspring is theirs. today we might struggle with monogamy and bore of it more quickly than men do, in the aggregate, for these reasons."

"Numerous studies suggest, it's not that women don't want to have sex. It's that they get bored more quickly from sex with a long-term partner."[xix]

What Do Cheaters Want?

I've discussed several types of affairs and some of the things that people are looking for when they cheat. But there are many other forms of cheating. The following are just a few more to consider.

A recent survey of Ashley Madison members[10] found that most people believe cheating encompasses more than just penis-in-vagina sex with someone other than your partner.

Fifty-five per cent of respondents agree that forming a deep emotional bond with someone other than your spouse is the number one form of cheating. Forty-four percent responded that the second most popular form of cheating is exchanging naked pictures. The same percentage think that exchanging erotic texts is also cheating.[xx]

According to Ashley Madison's director of communications, Isabella Mise, the definition of modern monogamy "is becoming more and more vague, so it really boils

---

10   Survey of 3,342 members of Ashley Madison between June 19, 2018 – July 8, 2018.

down to communication between couples and negotiating the terms of a marriage in an open way." Many people who cheat begin by talking about how unhappy they are with their marriage with someone outside the marriage, rather than with their spouse. And that "someone" is often found through social media. As Mise put it: "When couples aren't on the same page, or one partner simply isn't getting what they need, other options become desirable, even when that's as simple as finding someone to talk to."

What Constitutes Cheating?

According to an August 2018 survey[11] by Ashley Madison,[xxi] a cheating partner is someone who is:

Forming a deep emotional bond with someone else—55 percent

Sending naked pictures to someone other than me—46 percent

Texting erotic messages to someone other than me—44 percent

Maintaining an online dating profile—29 percent

Spending time with an ex-partner—29 percent

Casual flirting with someone other than me—18 percent

---

11   Survey of 2,767 members of Ashley Madison between June 19, 2018, and July 5, 2018.

Thinking about someone other than me
when having sex with me —18 percent
Going out to dinner with someone
of the opposite sex—18 percent
Communicating with an ex-partner—16 percent
Fantasizing about someone else—13 percent

The Repetitive Cheater

If you repeatedly seek out affairs, you may be someone who has difficulty with self-control, or you may be someone whose self-interest always comes first. This doesn't necessarily make you narcissistic; it just means you put your needs first, "as an automatic tendency." People who have more self-control can resist the tendency to cheat, even in situations where there is opportunity to do so— and if they have enough time to think about the potential consequences they can resist the impulse because of how it may affect them, and others, later on. [xxii]

To avoid cheating impulsively, you will need to stop before you cross that line and give some thought to the outcome, the fallout from the infidelity, and the way it will affect your sense of integrity afterwards. That is, how will you feel about yourself if you make the decision to cheat?

Make a clear and rational choice. Own your decision to act on the choice to cheat. If your decision is impulsive, you don't give yourself time to think about the lasting effects. Make the choice by clearly looking at your options. If you *want* to cheat, and have seriously considered all the consequences of the affair, then do it knowing you are fully responsible for your own actions. In this way, you may have less guilt afterwards and be less likely to blame other people. Be clear about your behaviors and choices, and take responsibility for your affair(s). You cross the line; no one makes you do it.

If it happened already and you regret it, is it time to decide if you should tell your partner?

The Emotional Affair

The "Emotional Affair" is a relationship with an intense level of intimacy and self-disclosure without direct sexual contact. In an emotional affair you may find you have a bond with the other person that feels romantic, but doesn't cross the line into something sexual. An emotional affair can be filled with deep longing for something more than friendship. It's not just a casual thing. You think about this person often and you wonder about a potential relationship. You confide in them, you turn to them with your secrets, you want to tell them everything. The emotional affair risks becoming even more of an intimate relationship than the one with your spouse.

Shirley Glass wrote in her now classic book on emotional affairs, *Not Just Friends,* [xxiii] that 44 percent of husbands and 57 percent of wives indicated that they have had an emotional affair—a relationship with a strong emotional attachment and without sexual intercourse—at some point in their lives.

The Slippery Slope

In the new crisis of infidelity, platonic friendships and workplace relationships are turning into emotional affairs, usually gradually, often without premeditation. Parties cross boundaries of emotional intimacy, sharing intimate information with a friend that has traditionally been the exclusive territory of a husband or wife. When these boundaries are overstepped, the relationship moves from friendship to a more emotional relationship and could ultimately lead to sexual infidelity. Even when the infidelity is "only" emotional, it often leads to a double life of deception and some type of sexual behaviors, threatening marriages that once felt secure.

If you recognize that your friendship or your partner's friendship may be in the danger zone of too much emotional intimacy, use this awareness to address concerns about your marriage. The following quiz from Shirley Glass's book[xxiv] will help you see where you stand.

Quiz: Has Your Friendship
Become an Emotional Affair?

1. Do you confide more to your friend than to your partner about how your day went?
2. Do you discuss negative feelings or intimate details about your marriage with your friend but not with your partner?
3. Are you open with your partner about the extent of your involvement with your friend?
4. Would you feel comfortable if your partner heard your conversation with your friend?
5. Would you feel comfortable if your partner saw a videotape of your meetings?
6. Are you aware of sexual tensions in this friendship?
7. Do you and your friend touch differently when you're alone than in front of others?
8. Are you in love with your friend?

Scoring key: You get one point each for yes to questions 1, 2, 6, 7, 8, and one point each for no to 3, 4, 5.

If you scored near 0, this is just a friendship.

If you scored 3 or more, you may not be "just friends."

If you scored 7 to 8, you are definitely involved in an emotional affair.

Entire books have been written on this type of relationship. The line I hear most often from people who justify their emotional cheating behavior is: "Yeah, I did it, but it didn't really count." If you have to say "it didn't really count," then it probably did. A *n emotional affair* counts as cheating.

The Online Affair

The "Online Affair" or "Cyber Affair" can be many things. An online affair can be a relationship in which each participant sends texts or photos of a sexual nature. It can include intimate chat sessions and erotically charged talks and escalate to mutual masturbation sessions with a webcam.

The online affair may be with a stranger who's really just an avatar. You may never know their real name or see an actual photo. On the internet, people can take on any persona—male or female, young or old—so for some it's indulging in a fantasy of anonymity. Online affairs feel safe for those who don't want to venture outside of a protective environment, or who are too apprehensive to have a real-life affair. Some even dismiss the idea of these online interactions as being true affairs because those engaging in them may never meet in person—there's no real skin-to-skin touching.

However, studies show that two-thirds of affairs

that start online will end up in real time, offline, with real sex.[xxv]

Because of the accessibility and anonymity of online cheating, it's easier than ever to indulge in sexual inter-action. Most internet porn sites are free (for some people viewing porn is a form of cheating, but for others it's only private masturbatory time and doesn't constitute a betrayal), and anyone can access porn online from their own laptop or smart phone while hanging out at the local coffee shop or library. It's easy to cover your tracks too, by hiding your browser history, or by using private "shad-ow" windows available on most browsers.

Sexual interaction in cyberspace means there'll be no "lipstick on the collar" confrontations and no receipts for hotel-room trysts. This reduced risk of being caught leads the online cheater to feel more confident and perhaps to be a little more reckless.

The risk with cyber affairs is how rapidly intimacy escalates; people are more likely to share personal details with someone online—perceived to be at a safe remove—than they are with friends and acquaintances they see on a regular basis.

When there's little-to-no face-to-face contact (and no eye-to-eye scrutiny) it's easier to reveal your deepest sexual fantasies. And this level of transparency and revelation quickly translates into feelings of deeper intimacy. It's a false sense of intimacy but it can feel rewarding to have someone listening; someone who seems to validate and empathize, particularly if you feel misunderstood and neglected at home.

The Allure of Infidelity

Some people "get off" on the naughtiness of cheating. They find it exciting, the thrill that comes with an affair is the thrill of doing something "wrong." Are you excited and turned on by the thought of having an affair—just by the illicitness of infidelity? Does the forbidden nature of infidelity make it irresistible for you or is your affair partner truly that alluring?

If the fear of getting caught is what makes it exciting for you, be sure to let your affair partner know. Be open and transparent about what makes the affair "hot" for you. Sometimes the point of an affair is to experience something you've been missing and have longed for. If your affair partner understands this, all the better—you'll get more of what you want. If they know what you find exciting, they may go along by heightening the tension to make it more fun. But you have to be honest about how you feel, and what you want. Don't mislead them about what you're really looking for.

They'll only know how to act out your desires and fantasies if you've communicated your needs. (Of course, before entering an affair you might consider asking your spouse to act out your fantasies. Would they do these things for you? Would they be willing to role-play if asked?)

If the real allure of having an affair, what really turns you on about cheating—is the clandestine nature of it, the fear of being caught—then you risk losing interest once time passes and it becomes safer and more predictable, and the fear or anxiety naturally decreases.

If you're a cheater who's *only* interested in the illicit nature of an affair, that means you probably won't want to leave your spouse for your affair partner. Make that clear upfront, so the person you are cheating with won't be under any illusion that you'll be divorcing your spouse and setting up house together.

Dialogue, communication and openness will help you to stay hot for the affair and forestall any attempts by your outside partner to push you to leave your spouse. Ironically, you have to act responsibly in the affair—just as you should in a marriage—to maintain the excitement. That means being open and honest about what you want.

Let's Talk About the Tough Stuff

In our society we continue to view affairs as a symptom of dysfunctional marriages. But that one-size-fits-all view of affairs doesn't align with our current model of adultery. After decades of studies, as mentioned previously, we know that many affairs happen within well-functioning marriages, to otherwise "normal," even happy, couples.

Most cheaters aren't sociopathic and don't set out to lie to their partner. I'm betting that you didn't wake up this morning and say to yourself, "Let's see how I can hurt my spouse today!" (If you did, you have more problems than this book can help you with; please seek out professional help immediately.)

However, sometimes there are underlying issues that lead you to cheat—emotional or mental health issues that need to be addressed. If you are depressed, addicted, anxious, have a trauma history, or have other serious things happening in your life, therapy can help. Find a therapist who is empathetic and can help you talk through your problems and what led you to cheat.

There may be tough issues from your childhood that are being triggered emotionally now. If you have old traumas that are surfacing, you may need professional help to heal. Give yourself the time and attention you deserve to work through your past. Before you bring old traumas into the present, get help and take care of yourself. You may find that the rewards of having a trained professional to talk to can relieve you of stress you didn't even know you were carrying.

Coercion

We can't have a book about cheating without talking about the drastic inequities among men and women that persist in society and in the workplace.

Some people (mostly women, but also men) have extramarital sex because they've been coerced. They end up in affairs, feeling powerless to resist a man or woman who holds sway over their workplace. They relent to the pressure to have sex rather than suffer negative consequences to their career or to their personal lives.

Film-industry directors and producers have seduced and preyed upon young actors for a hundred years. Judges, priests, coaches, athletes, executives, and academics all have a long history of coercing, pressuring, threatening or even blackmailing women and men into sexual relationships.

The much-publicized rise of the #MeToo movement, a reaction to systemic sexual harassment and abuse within the entertainment industry, has led to a groundswell of similar revelations, protests and lawsuits in other industries, and could mark a sea change in the treatment of (mostly) women—in particular—in the workplace.

If you're a man or a woman who's applying any form of coercion, using your position or power in any way to engage in sex with an employee or colleague: you need to stop! You aren't a cheater, you're a sexual predator—another category altogether, and one that demands you seek immediate therapy. If you have forced a woman or a man to have sex against their will, this is abuse and even rape. The consequences are steep, for the victim of your sexual predation, and for you.

If you are the one being coerced, if someone in a position of power is pressuring you into a sexual act or relationship, or if you feel trapped in your affair, seek help from legal counsel, and a mental health counselor or trauma therapist.

Now let's move on.

Endnotes

x https://www.ncbi.nlm.nih.gov/pubmed/21152404

xi 2014 study https://www2.psy.uq.edu.au/~uqbziets/Zietsch et al 2014
Genetic analysis of extrapair mating.pdf

xii Hastings, Nick, Carter, Sue, Harbaugh, Caroll, Winslow, James, A role
for central vasopressin in pair bonding in monogamous prairie voles,
Nature volume 365, pages 545–548 (07 October 1993)

xiii Martin, Wednesday (2018) *Untrue: Why Nearly Everything We Believe
About Women, Lust, and Infidelity Is Wrong and How the New Science
Can Set Us Free, Harper Collins, NY NY*

xiv 2014 study https://www2.psy.uq.edu.au/~uqbziets/Zietsch percent20et
percent20al percent202014 percent20Genetic percent20analysis percen-
t20of percent20extrapair percent20mating.pdf

xv https://www.psychologytoday.com/us/blog/in-the-name-love/200811/pro-
claimed-monogamy-clandestine-adultery

xvi Ben-Zeev, Aaron, (2004) Love Online, Emotions on the Internet, Cambridge University Press

xvii Perel, Esther (2018) State of Affairs, Harper Collins, NY, NY

xviii Diamond, Lisa (2009) Sexual Fluidity, Harvard University Press,
Boston MA

xix https://www.menshealth.com/sex-women/a23301786/wednesday-mar-
tin-untrue/

xx https://www.fromgirltogirl.com/new-study-55-say-emotional-bond-is-
cheating-ashley-madison/

xxi https://www.fromgirltogirl.com/new-study-55-say-emotional-bond-is-
cheating-ashley-madison/

xxii Shaul Shalvi, Ori Eldar, Yoella Bereby-Meyer Honesty Requires Time
(and Lack of Justifications) SAGE Journals First Published September
12, 2012 Research Article

xxiii Glass, Shirley, (2004) *Not Just Friends,* Emotional Affairs, Atria Books

xxiv *REF: This quiz by Shirley P. Glass was first printed in USA Today (June 20, 1988) in an article by Karen Peterson, "When platonic relationships get too close for comfort," p. 6D. Taken from the book NOT "Just Friends", ©2018 Dr. Shirley Glass

xxv *Journal of Marital and Family Therapy* (Vol. 34, No. 4) 2008 Hertlein

CHAPTER SIX
Sometimes It's a Mistake

"I am not married. Just because I am in a relationship with a married man, that doesn't make me a cheater!" Mary said. She sat in my office and cried, refusing to believe that she was partly to "blame" for the affair she found herself in with a married man, Raf.

She had been in a relationship with him for four years. She had no interest in getting married and she felt content, most of the time, with their setup. "He calls me on Thursdays and Sundays, and we get together every Monday during the day and he sleeps over on Tuesdays. That's enough for me. I spend holidays with my mother, she lives far away. This way I don't have anyone telling me what to do or tying me down. I mean I love Raf, but I don't need a husband. He can stay with his wife for all I care."

But there had been a new development in their triangulated relationship. Raf's wife was pregnant. "This changes things," I said to Mary. "How do you feel about dating a married man with a pregnant wife?"

"I feel bad for her," Mary said. "I never really thought about her as a real person. But now I find I am counting down the weeks of her pregnancy. She is 15 weeks pregnant now. How can Raf be with me when she is pregnant with his child? Now I think about having my own kid. Maybe I do want a kid of my own. I don't know."

Raf filled Mary's sexual needs and made her life feel complete. But now, with Raf and his wife expecting a child, she began to realize that his wife was a real person, not just a distant idea. She didn't want to be responsible for breaking up their family if the affair was revealed.

But she was angry at Raf. How could she deal with her own feelings?

What is Happiness?

An affair doesn't necessarily create long-term happiness. Relationships are developmental in nature; we tend to want to move things along, to get to the next level, and to grow as a couple. And yet an affair can have a self-defined limit. Sometimes an affair can't go anywhere beyond where or what it is.

Only about 3 percent of cheaters marry the person they cheat with—a very small percentage.[xxvi] Most cheaters don't leave their spouses for their affair partners—

perhaps because unhappiness is not always the cause of affairs. It's likely, then, that if your cheating partner is happy being married, they'll stay put. However, there are always exceptions to this "rule."

Interview with Cara

I spoke to Cara, a sixty-year-old woman who volunteered to talk with me about her affairs. She started off the conversation by telling me "I hate the word cheating. It implies that we are doing something terrible, like cheating on our taxes, or breaking a legal contract. An affair is something that you do because you need to; it's not like you are stealing from a store or something."

I asked Cara if she had a better word for "cheating" or "affair" but she said she couldn't come up with anything. I wondered why she had such a strong reaction to the words, and I asked if she felt like people judged "cheaters."

"Yes, of course, and I don't feel like I am doing anything wrong. My husband and I grew apart. We didn't have sex for over six years. There was some mental illness involved, he had depression, and anxiety. So, I went online and I met some other men. I had to take care of myself. It is not like I was robbing him of anything."

I asked her about what happened and she said that

when her husband eventually found out, he "cleaned out the bank accounts and disappeared." Cara was left broke and alone. Which, according to her, didn't feel all that different than when she and her husband had been living together.

Cara continued to date online, choosing to meet married men who were traveling through the area where she lived, instead of men who lived in her town. The men she met were pilots and professors, speakers and businessmen. They wanted only short-term sexual liaisons and that worked for her, for a while. But then there was one man in her town, a married man, who she talked with online. They chatted by email for almost two years, before she finally agreed to meet him in person.

"I didn't want to get involved with someone in my own town. If it didn't work out, I was afraid to run into him in the grocery store." But they did finally meet for coffee and from there the friendship slowly grew into something more physical. "He stayed married. I was the other woman for a long time. He didn't want to end his marriage. His wife was tough. She suspected but she wouldn't divorce him. Our relationship lasted that way for a long time. I was okay with it. I didn't trust him totally. I wasn't ready to get married again, I didn't trust that he wasn't going to hurt me the way my husband had."

Cara stayed in the relationship with her married boyfriend for over five years. Finally, when his wife found out, he left his marriage. Today he and Cara live together in her house, while he continues to struggle through a difficult divorce.

Attachment and Companionship

Passion can diminish over time, whether in a marriage or in an affair. Routine and responsibility strengthen attachment and companionship in relationships. But attachment and companionship can be total passion killers.

In any new relationship, in a marriage or outside a marriage, we judge our initial interest based on our attraction to the other person. If we pursue the relationship, we look for personality traits such as compassion and trustworthiness to ensure that this is someone we can partner with and share our most intimate selves and, perhaps, create a family. Once we've established this trustworthiness, only then do we let ourselves become attached. Eventually, as we become increasingly comfortable with this person, we relax into something I call "the sweatpants phase of a relationship." We've finally met someone with whom we can be totally relaxed.

But that feeling of security and safety is separate from eroticism.

The erotically charged part of a relationship is the aspect of a relationship where passion lives; the flirting and sexual excitement that makes us feel truly in love—not just loving and being cosy together on the couch in front of the television—but the feeling of being passionately in love.

If we make it through all the potential hurdles in a new relationship, including meeting each other's friends and family, sickness, arguments, and living and travelling together—then eventually our attachment strengthens. We share more life experiences, become more familiar (more *family*), as we become more connected. We reveal more about ourselves and our history and dreams and fears; we truly get to know each other. But this bond of attachment doesn't, somewhat surprisingly, lead to better sex. In fact, it's more likely that the *safer you feel* with one another, the *less erotic* the relationship becomes.

You'd think it would be the opposite: that the more secure you feel with your partner the more vulnerable you could be with each other, sharing sexual fantasies and engaging in sexy adventures—taking erotic risks, shaking things up in your sex life. But there's a risk to shaking things up.

The longer you are together, the closer you are to one another, the harder it becomes to talk about your real sexual fantasies and desires. You're nervous about what they might think—you don't want to scare them away and risk being rejected for your desires, and perhaps losing the relationship you have.

In the beginning you might have less concern about their reaction to your sexual proclivities. You don't have as much to lose then. And the sex is more selfish in the beginning, too. You think more about your own pleasure, your own orgasm. Now you worry more about their desire, their arousal. What are they thinking? What do they want? Do they still want you?

In order to create a more passionate relationship, you have to work on the erotic part as much, if not more, than your companionship. You have to put your sex life first and share your fantasies and desires. You *have* to take risks.

Wednesday Martin refers to the work of psychologist Marta Meana, one expert whose studies have shown that "Long term relationships are particularly hard on female desire…" [the preceding is a quote from Meana. This next sentence is me paraphrasing her and the literature, i think, so should not be in quotes to be safe: in the aggregate, men seem to be better at wanting what they already have; for women, it is more of a struggle. "[xxvii]

If your marriage is no longer passionate, and you're

bored or feeling neglected, it's not uncommon to seek outside erotic energy instead of working on what's missing in your life.

What's Wrong?

What's wrong with you if you cheat?

Possibly nothing. It could just be that you are a disrupter. Seeking an affair is a way to shake things up, to find new energy in your life. To feel sexy or sexual. To feel wanted. To find excitement or challenge or love. But if *you choose to cheat*, you're definitely causing a problem. Not because of who you are, but because of what you are doing.

Let's assume there's *nothing wrong with you*. And let's assume that, just maybe—and this is important—*this wasn't a mistake*. Maybe this was the best thing that could have happened for you—and ultimately—even your spouse. And for your lover, too, and for your job—maybe even for your kids.

Only you can figure this out.

Is it a mistake?

Once a Cheater, Always a Cheater?

"Once a cheater, always a cheater," the maxim goes. But is there any truth to this? And what really makes someone a serial cheater?

According to data collected by the American *Journal of Marital and Family Therapy*, 57 percent of men and 54 percent of women reported that they cheated.[12] The University of Chicago statistics from over twenty five years ago indicate that 40% of men and 20% of women cheated.[13] But there's no indication in this study that once any of them have begun, they're addicted and stuck in a pattern of cheating, or even that they have the "personality of a cheater." Studies can't make judgements about cheaters, nor can counselors, unless they meet them in person during ongoing therapy sessions. And without the proper training, it's doubtful that spouses can make any judgements, either.[xxviii]

---

12   Joan D. Atwood PhD & Limor Schwartz MA (2002) Cyber-Sex, Journal of Couple & Relationship Therapy, 1:3, 37-56, DOI: 10.1300/J398v01n03_03

13   Kristina Coop Gordon Donald H. Baucom Douglas K. Snyder (2004) An Integrative Intervention For Promoting Recovery From Extramarital Affairs, Journal of Marriage and Family therapy **Volume30, Issue2** April 2004 Pages 213-231

It's also unwise for cheaters to slap a label or diagnosis on themselves. As it is, in the field of treatment for sex and couple's therapy, there's discord among professionals about repetitive cheating. Some therapists are quick to label cheaters who have repetitive affairs as "sex addicts," while other clinicians refute that label and deny its accuracy.

Are You a Sex Addict?

Sex is a Behavior, not a substance. For most of us, sex enables the greatest pleasure the human body can experience. Which is why we can be driven to experience that pleasure repeatedly, and in a myriad of ways.

The World Health Organization defines **sexually compulsive behaviors** as an "*inability to control intense sexual urges*," leading people to neglect their health, despite a "*lack of pleasure or satisfaction*" from the behaviors. However, among certified sex therapists and many other professionals in the medical community, there's been much controversy about labeling or diagnosing sex as an addiction.

There are many licensed counselors who do a wonderful job with people suffering from out-of-control sexual behaviors. But the risk for cheaters seeking help is that almost anyone can hang out a shingle and declare themselves a therapist for "sex addicts." Some are good.

Others use guilt and shame as a way to "treat" the cheater. Unfortunately, some cheaters may find themselves being incorrectly diagnosed and shamed around sex.

That doesn't mean that you should excuse or ignore any obsessive, compulsive, self-harming, repetitive sexual behaviors. Get help if you need it; go to a harm reduction therapist or seek a sex therapist trained in the area of erotic recovery.[14]

If sex between two people —whether marital or extramarital—is consensual and mutually pleasurable, all judgement surrounding it should be discarded.

Get help and support from a therapist if you need it for anxiety, depression, trauma and other issues you may be struggling with immediately but don't hesitate to "vet" your therapist, which means talk by phone or email first, then go to two or three sessions before you decide you want to continue.

---

14   A warning: If you become a danger to yourself or others, go to an emergency room immediately. Sex can be, at best, an act of pleasure and a vehicle for intimacy. At worst, sex can be used as a weapon to perpetrate an act of violence.

What's "Normal"?

There is no "normal" when it comes to how much or what kind of sex you should be having. These estimates and definitions are based purely on the other people's sexual preferences and experiences.

Studies of averages, however, do exist. One study, for instance, shows that couples married more than four years have sex twice to three times per week. After about ten years, that average decreases to three or four times per month. But these averages aren't indicators of what's "normal." They're simply an indication of the results found from *one* study of *one* group of respondents.

So, what is a healthy sex life? It's one in which sex is *"safe, sane and consensual."* This is a phrase commonly used among the BDSM (bondage, discipline, dominance & submission, and sadomasochism) community—a community in which practitioners are encouraged to comply with those three expectations when engaging in acts of role-playing. "Safe sex" means that the sex does not put either of you in danger. The use of condoms to protect each of you from sexually transmitted infections (STIs) would be included in this category. "Sane sex" means the sex is not pathologically violent or dangerous; you're not putting your partner in physical or psychological danger as part of the sexual experience. And all sex acts should be "consensual sex," where each partner can clearly and freely agree to anything that happens between them.

Following the guidelines of safety, sanity and consensuality in sex should help to offset any negative judgements surrounding your sexual practices—no matter how "unconventional" some may consider them. And do note: if a professional, friend or acquaintance suggests you're having "too much" sex, it may be because you're having more sex than the person judging you, or if they deem it "abnormal" it may be because it's a different "type" of sex than the sex they're engaging in.

Affairs have traditionally been seen as subversive, anti-authoritarian and against the moral norm of a monogamous society. Rory Bahadur, author of an Elon Law Review article about sexual morality,[xxix] says that "Judeo-Christian norms are the bases of our sexual morality, and these norms are reflected in the law regulating consensual adult sexual activity. Reinforced by the law, these norms perpetuate an environment where nonconformance to the standards results in feelings of shame.... [T]here simply is no empirical basis for this morality and ... complying with this morality [has] perpetuated a history of discrimination, cruelty, and female suppression. As a result, these norms should not be the basis of our sexual morality."[15]

In other words, *all judgment around sex is projection*, based on cultural, religious and moral beliefs.

Affairs and Guilt

A man called José wrote to me after I posted a blog about the difficulties of *making up our minds* when we are in an affair. In the blog post, I wrote about how, sometimes, we make up stories about the affair and have visions about how great life would be if we could live with our affair partners full time. We've "made up our mind," and *think* we know exactly what we want but are prevented from making changes due to circumstances beyond our control. Other times, "making up our minds" means deciding, for the first time, what our thoughts and feelings really are, without any input from another person.

José wrote: "I have been having an affair with a woman I met at church. She and I were texting for about six months. I am divorced, and was ready to get serious with this woman. She said we would be together. She would end her marriage. Then instead, she ended it with me because she felt guilty. I didn't hear from her for a

---

15   Badhour says: "Western sexual morality says "…The biting of the apple is widely regarded as a metaphor for Eve satisfying her sexual desire or lust with one other than Adam. "[

while but I kept texting her. And then her husband contacted me and told me he found my texts. He was upset and told me to stop contacting her. I never heard from her again.

"I still feel the guilt of this. I guess I am still carrying a torch for her. I betrayed her by texting with her when I knew she was married. I was supposed to be a good guy. But I thought she would leave her husband for me. I regret the whole thing although I still would like to make things right between us. I was an idiot for believing that she wanted to be with me.... I guess I was naive."

José's remorse is common. I asked him why he was so tough on himself. He said "Because I got involved with a woman who promised she would leave her husband and then she changed her mind." José's lesson, he said, was "...don't ever text something that the other person will have to erase. It's not fair to them. Even if you think the relationship will last and you will end up together, you never know."

When José's affair ended, he went into a "shame spiral." He could not hold his head up at church and felt like his world was falling apart. He had to grieve the affair. He had put himself into a vulnerable place with the married woman and she had rejected him. He needed to talk about what he really felt. Therapy helped him to examine his feelings, and commit to himself that he would learn to communicate in any relationship in the future.

Not all affairs end this way. Some last for years. Some end when the single partner decides they want a more permanent relationship. Or they reach a more organic conclusion.

When is Your Guilt a Sign of a Real Problem?

If you have ongoing concerns about your own behavior—for instance, if you've tried to stop having ongoing or multiple sexual relationships that interfere with your work or your health and are unable to do so, or if your sexual behavior has gotten you into trouble with the law but you continue to repeat those same behaviors—then you may be struggling with an underlying mental health condition.

Sometimes anxiety or a history of trauma can lead to unchecked and potentially harmful sexual behavior—obsessively cheating, for instance, or being on a constant hunt for fresh sexual experiences as a way of distracting yourself from your real, unprocessed feelings.

If it seems like your alcohol or substance abuse is out of control, then it is time to get help right away. Go to www.aa.org for help. It's important to stabilize your life as soon as possible, and the only way to do that is to stop or substantially reduce your substance abuse or other self-harming behavior. Go to www.AASECT.org for a list of Certified Sex Therapists in your area.

Is Cheating Natural?

Affairs affect approximately one out of three couples—that's one-third of all couples. Most of the literature on affair recovery assumes infidelity is just a symptom of fundamental problems within a marriage or committed partnership. However, that assumption ignores the greater dilemma: is monogamy the exception rather than the norm? It might be that the ideal of monogamy is an impossibly high standard for the average person—or even that monogamy itself counters human nature.

If it is human nature to seek out sex with multiple partners, then wouldn't we all be having affairs? And wouldn't affairs make us happier? As it is, only one third of us cheat, while half of us continue to enter what we hope will be monogamous marriages—even after divorce. Something isn't adding up.

Cheating doesn't seem to be the answer to our marriage woes. Affairs, statistically, don't make us happy in the long run, and most cheaters don't spend very much time in their affairs. Ten percent of extramarital infidelities last just one day (or night). Another 10 percent of infidelities or affairs last less than one month; and the rest last, at the most, a year or two. Few affairs last longer than four years.[xxx]

So, if the average affair lasts less than two years, does that mean affairs are ultimately dissatisfying, or does it mean they're doing exactly what they're meant to do? And if so, what is that exactly?

Are Affairs the Answer to Long-Term Happiness?

Affairs make us happy, but only temporarily.

As a reminder, we live in a culture in which 50 percent of marriages end in divorce. And many of those who divorce remarry a second and even a third time. Second marriages end in divorce at an even higher rate: almost 70 percent. The divorce rate for third marriages is higher still.

In 2013, four out of ten new marriages included at least one partner who had been married previously. Many of these marriages end because of infidelity.

Are affairs only the result of our failure at marriage? Maybe we're just really bad at life-long commitment. It could be that monogamy is just too dull and routine and too difficult to uphold in a society and culture that demands eternal happiness.

Perpetual Vetting

Alicia Walker, Assistant Professor of Sociology at Missouri State and Author of *The Secret Life of the Cheating Wife*[16] took a massive survey of cheaters that focused on both men and women and published the interviews with the women. I talked to Dr. Walker about her experience.

"These women [in the study] were articulate – gregarious – funny, storytellers, women I would want to know," she said. For the most part, Walker realized, the women who were in affairs had "…great clarity, what they were trying to accomplish made sense – they said things like, "I'm not getting enough sex" and "there are not enough orgasms in my life.""

The men, she told me, did not seem as light hearted and didn't use as much humor. They talked more about what Walker described as "what was really going on – they had "lost emotional intimacy in their marriages." The men said things like, "my wife doesn't care who I am as a person," "she doesn't care about my day," "she is so busy with herself," "I am not getting as much attention," and "there is nothing left over for me."

The men seemed to want someone to lavish them with attention, who remembered that they had a haircut, a meeting that day at work. The women said they currently

---

16   Alicia Walker, Assistant Professor of Sociology at Missouri State and Author of *The Secret Life of the Cheating Wife*

had good partners, good fathers, good relationships, almost all of them had their emotional needs currently met in their marriage. They were looking for sex and erotic charge in their affairs.

The men showed that their affairs were a symptom of a larger problem – the spark was lost in their marriage; the intimacy was gone, they said that they had lost interest in each other – the affairs were about seeking "someone who was happy to see him; happy to talk to him; interested in them as a person."[17]

Just like my own experience on Ashley Madison, when I had a profile as Tom, and one as Tina, I found that these stories represented a surprising polar opposite of what we assume people are looking for in affairs. Men were looking for intimacy, for attention, for relationships, for companionship and women were interested in eroticism, in passion - in better, or more of a sex life.

"It was interesting," Walker said. "Although we could not determine how the profile of someone who with premeditation and calculation would seek out an affair compared or correlated with the cheater who would have a tryst at the office or would get involved with a neighbor, I suspect that consciously or unconsciously people must

---

17   Personal interview with Alicia Walker

be drawing the experience to them."

I asked her if she thought that more people were cheating now than ever before, because of the ease of access to online sites like Ashley Madison and other dating websites.

What she said surprised me. "I don't know how we would ever know if the rates [of cheating] have ever increased – it's tempting to think perhaps it has increased because of the ease with which we can – we carry around a little computer in our pockets – is this a real increase or a shift in how we are doing it? If people didn't have the option to cheat online would they be cheating in their off line lives? I'm not sure if it's increased."

"What we do know," she said, "is that affairs are un-derreported." Are women cheating in greater numbers? Maybe not. What we do know is that they are telling us that they're doing it in greater numbers because they have less to lose. "Because they are perhaps more or less inclined to leave their marriages – they make more money so it's less of a disaster if they leave; we have to assume the rates are far greater than we ever realized."

What surprised her about her study? She had set up a survey thinking that women cheaters had a spouse and then, in addition, had a single affair partner. But what she discovered was that her thinking was wrong. She explained that a woman would have a main partner – a spouse - and also multiple other partners –the women were not replicating monogamy in an affair partner – this was a big surprise. The women said things like, "I have been married – all my eggs in one basket – but for my pleasure, for my sexual needs, I am going outside the marriage – if it hasn't worked out with one guy why would I do that same thing again? Why would I think that would work out?"

Walker calls this "perpetual vetting," or having "play mates," the idea is to keep several active affairs going at all times. The men cheaters, on the other hand, all talked about having just one affair partner – they all wanted a partner to "just want them." The men wanted to talk every day, on the phone, by text, etc. to their affair partners.

I found this to be true as well. The men that reached out to me when I was online also said they wanted to be in constant contact. This was important to them. They were creating parallel relationships to the relationships they had with their wives.

The women were more ambivalent. The women in affairs told Walker things like, "Yeah I probably would talk every day but more often than not it would be just 'hi how are you doing,' a quick check in." Whereas the men were more about "she needs to make time for me; she needs to be interested in my daily life."

Walker's take away from her study? "The more I listened the more I found that infidelity is anything but simple. As much as we want to think cheaters are bad people, with a moral flaw, that is not what I found."

Endnotes

xxvi Spring, Janis, (2018) After the Affair, Harper Collins Publisher, rere-leased 2018

xxvii Martin, Wednesday, 2018, *UNTRUE: Why Nearly Everything We Believe About Women, Lust, and Adultery is Wrong and How the New Science Can Set Us Free*

xxviii https://www.statisticbrain.com/infidelity-statistics/] [https://www.apa.org/pubs/journals/features/cfp-0000012.pdf][Couple and Family Psychology: Research and Practice © 2014 American Psychological Association 2014, Vol. 3, No. 1, 1–12 2160-4096/14/$12.00 DOI: 10.1037/cfp0000012 Infidelity and Behavioral Couple Therapy: Relationship Outcomes Over 5 Years Following Therapy Rebeca A. Marín Andrew Christensen University of Washington University of California Los Angeles David C. Atkins University of Washington

xxix Bahadur Rory Individual Sovereignty, Freer Sex, And Diminished Privacy: How An Informed And Realistic Modern Sexual Morality Provides Salvation From Unjustified Shame Elon.Edu (https://www.elon.edu/e/CmsFile/GetFile?FileID=551)

xxx Spring, Janis

CHAPTER SEVEN
Sometimes You Fall in Love

When You're the Other Woman or Man and Single

If you're the other man or woman, *and* unattached and you are cheating with a married partner, you may be facing your own unique challenges. Being single and cheating with an attached partner has its benefits and its complexities. You have your own questions about your affair and possibly your own choices to make about your future.

Being with someone who is married can feel exciting, but it can also be damaging to your ego. It can boost your self-esteem one moment and send your confidence plummeting in another. Sometimes in the same day.

A married partner may be convenient for you in many ways if you aren't looking for a committed or monogamous relationship. This is obviously true for many single cheaters, hence the popularity of married-dating sites. Your relationship may be exactly what works for you; just enough commitment, not too much interaction, a titrated level of intimacy and the perfect kind of attachment for you right now, at this moment in your life.

But if you are in love with a fantasy, imagining a future with your married partner, you may spend a lot of your waking hours spinning potential outcomes in your mind. And you may find that you are beating yourself up emotionally, for wishing that things were different. Or you may be waiting for things to change. If you are wondering if it's time to make some changes, here are some things to think about.

Do you really see your partner for who they are? Are you in love with them, or is it the unavailability of your affair partner that makes them so attractive? If they were to become a full-time lover or spouse, would you have the same feelings for them?

Spring says: "I've seen so many couples break up … once they're free to be with each other. When you're in love, you only see the fantasy, the positive side, and you're often blind to how this new person will annoy or hurt you." xxxi

Sometimes the fantasy is simply a feeling, a longing for someone that you can't have. Are you longing for something that is never going to be more than it is right now? If it isn't going to be anything more than it is now, can you accept it for what it is?

Just Enough

Not all cheaters are married. They're simply adults in relationships with other adults. They're unattached but have chosen to be in a relationship with someone who is attached.

If this is you, you might be getting exactly what you need from this relationship. Maybe you don't want more than your married partner can give you. Maybe you don't want every weekend, every holiday together, or you don't want children. Maybe you're just fine, in fact, without the commitment of a monogamous relationship.

But then again, maybe you're not fine. Maybe you're in a relationship with someone who tells you that more is coming. That they're going to leave their partner, that they really want to be with you and that they want to marry you.

And so, you wait. And it seems, at first, like things are going well. They make a move to tell their spouse. They have long, heartfelt conversations with you about what the future will look like when they leave. They might even make an effort toward separation or divorce.

But they stay in the marriage, and don't divorce.

They don't even separate from their spouse because they can't bring themselves to leave. Maybe it's just too painful. Maybe there are kids involved and they can't "tear apart the family." Or maybe they never really planned to end it at all.

As previously noted, married people do cheat even when their primary relationship is healthy. They're satisfied at home yet still seek out an affair: and you're that affair. So now you're getting *some* of the things that you want and need. But you were hoping for more and keep wishing that things would change.

Or, you're settling and just take what you've been given.

Anna, 42, was fresh from her divorce. She reveled in her newfound freedom. "I do what I want. I go out with my friends; and I have a new boyfriend."

When her married boyfriend, David, could get away, he and Anna had sex, watched movies, or he fixed things around her house.

As far as Anna was concerned, it was David's choice alone to cheat on his wife, and she didn't judge him for that choice. She herself felt very little guilt about the affair—she wasn't the one who was married—and she was in no hurry to enter a committed relationship. She enjoyed his company and, for now, she had what she needed.

David came over to be with her when he could, she said. She had no interest in having him around too often, she liked her freedom, and she didn't want another husband. "I don't want him complaining to me, I don't want him to sleep here every night. I love my life just the way it is. Why do people have to judge me for my choices? I am getting exactly what I want. I don't need or want anything beyond this. If I did, or when I do, I will end it. But I get to make that decision. No one else. For once in my life I have the freedom to make the choices I want. Including staying up late, sleeping till noon, wearing my pajamas all day. No one else tells me what to do. I love it."

The Third Wheel

You may or may not feel responsible if you're dating a cheater. If they're married, they've made the decision to cheat on their spouse.

But, let's be clear. This isn't just dating; it's an affair, and most likely one that's fraught with tension and stress. We've all heard the clichés of what to expect when a single person is involved with a married one—lonely nights, weekends on your own. And, over time, resentment and anger. If you're the other man or woman, your relationship is stigmatized; and so is your role in the relationship. People assume you are the jealous lover who'll never get over the affair, or the angry third wheel who resents the spouse.

But being the third person in a cheating triangle is more complex than that. Many "third wheels" like Anna are comfortable in their status, and don't go mad from loneliness or revenge. Some choose to remain single and prefer the low demands that come with affairs. They're not responsible for their lover's needs, and relish the joy of a thrilling sexual relationship with little commitment.

The Single Cheater

John, a "third wheel" or "single cheater" came to me for therapy. His current affair partner, Aaron, wanted to leave his husband to be with John.

John revealed that he didn't want that to happen. "I like my apartment, it's perfect for just me, alone. I like living alone. I've never asked Aaron for more than what we have right now. Aaron assumes I want more."

I asked John if he had talked to Aaron about his feelings. "I have, but he doesn't listen, he has a fantasy that I want him to leave his husband. I have no interest in that."

John liked being single and, he said, "If Aaron wants to hurt his husband by telling him about our affair, that's his business, but I did not sign up for that. This is *not* what I signed up for at all. I like being the single guy in an affair. But if he feels guilty I understand. But I don't want a committed, long-term relationship right now."

Being Cheated on When you're the Cheater

What if your cheating partner cheats on you? Just because you cheat doesn't mean someone can't cheat on you. Just because you're in an open relationship, cheating happens even then. How can you avoid this situation, or worse, repeating it? Because let's face it, no one likes being cheated on.

Being Cheated on Makes You Stronger?

"Higher mating intelligence" means a cheated-on person is better able to "detect cues" in her future mates. After a break-up, she'll be able to spot the red flags in her next relationship; identifying signs that indicate "low mate value," such as avoidance, obfuscation, lying and sneaking around—all of the cheating behaviors she's become familiar with. She might even be able to quickly pick out "another cheater across a crowded room," and, if she wants to, turn around and walk the other way.[xxxii]

Sometimes it takes years and many experiences to adapt and nurture this kind of personal growth. Other times, it only takes one relationship. If you're with someone who's cheated on you in the past, or who cheated on a previous partner, you need to take time to reflect. Here are a few things to consider...

Choosing Wisely

1) On a scale of one to ten, how would you score this person's general integrity?

2) Can you think of three examples of why you should or shouldn't trust this person?

3) Can you think of three red flags in this relationship you've been ignoring?

4) If a friend were in this relationship, would you advise them to end the affair?

5) What does your intuition tell you about this relationship?

After you've answered all these questions ask yourself:

"Why am I in a relationship with this person?"

"Can this person be trusted? If not, why am I with them?"

"Am I ignoring any red flags in this relationship?"

"If I would tell a friend to get out of this relationship, why the heck am I still in it?

"What have I learned from this exercise?"

How *Do* You End an Affair?

What if, while reading this book, you've come to the realization that you want out of the affair? This affair you've been having might have seemed like a good idea at first, but now things have become too complicated. And you don't know how to begin extricating yourself.

If you want out, there's a good way and a bad way to end it. Ending your affair with integrity - compassion for yourself and everyone involved - allows you a chance at healing: healing your past, and, perhaps giving yourself some time for thinking about the future – maybe even your next relationship.

It also means being responsible for the relationship you have had with your affair partner. Ending things with integrity means dealing with the consequences of all of your actions. It's time to take responsibility and handle the fallout, and stepping up to your new life. It means facing things like an adult.

It's really quite simple. Step One: understand that you owe your affair partner much more than an apology. "Sorry, I made a mistake," may not be enough. The two of you shared what was most likely a sexual and/or an emotional relationship. It was probably exciting and maybe even fun, and you both risked a lot to steal some pleasurable moments. You probably shared many things, including dreams of a possible future together, maybe the promise of a life beyond the affair. Whatever you discussed, the two of you created some kind of a bond. There will likely be pain once it's broken, so you need to lessen that hurt as much as you can.

Step Two: take a hard look at the kind of ending conversation that will entail.

Questions to Ask Yourself

Questions to ask yourself about your ending conversation:

1) Did you lead your affair partner to believe that you had feelings for them?
2) Did you text, email and/or call them on a regular basis?
3) Did you have sex with your affair partner more than once?
4) Did you promise your affair partner that you would end your marriage for them?
5) Did you tell your affair partner that you loved them?

If you answered "yes" to any of these five questions, you need to end this affair with integrity.

Don't underestimate the impact you have made on this

person's life. You were involved in their life and got them involved in yours. You owe them this.

Why Can't I Just Ghost?

One: If you just stop texting them or taking their calls (that is, you "ghost" them by essentially evaporating from their lives), your "ghosted" affair partner could show up in your life unexpectedly, at your home or office, in an attempt to talk things out, or to confront you to get some answers. This could make things very awkward, and lead to unwanted consequences.

Two: Simply ghosting, or disappearing, has the potential to create ongoing hurt and betrayal. In their desire for closure, your affair partner could drag out contact with you in the hope of continuing the affair or simply to find resolution.

Three: If you've ended contact abruptly, with no explanation, there's a chance your affair partner will want revenge and could contact your spouse or other family members, or your boss or friends. Their aim could be to create chaos in your life, just as you've done in theirs.

Four: Don't ghost. Instead, end the affair with integrity; it's the right thing to do. Be responsible in your actions and treat your affair partner with compassion and respect. You owe them an explanation when you make the decision to break off the affair, because it's the right thing, the adult thing, to do.

Ending Your Affair with Integrity

So, you're ready to have the conversation. But how do you do it? You are nervous. You aren't sure how they're going to react. You want to do it well; you don't want to ghost. Here's a guide to ending your affair, and some ways to do it.

Rules of Disengagement

1) Make an Appointment. Ask your affair partner for some time to talk… in person.
2) Be clear when you meet. Let them know that you are ending your affair.
3) Take responsibility; don't blame or make excuses.. Tell them you feel badly about hurting them, leading them on, or getting them into this relationship in the first place. Tell them that you feel responsible for their partner's pain as well.
4) Show empathy. Try to relate to how they are feeling, take responsibility for your part in the affair.

"I imagine you're hurt, angry, relieved, confused. I wish I...."

5) Set boundaries. Make sure you're clear about what you will and won't continue to do. "I will continue to care about you, but I can no longer speak on the phone or answer emails."

6) Establish rules. If you are having an affair with someone at work you may need to establish new rules for office behavior. "I'll try to maintain a 'light and polite' relationship, but I can no longer have personal discussions or share feelings at work."

7) Admit your ambivalence. It's okay to be honest. "I have to end things, but of course I have regrets and I feel ambivalent. But this is really over now."

8) Express appreciation. Tell them you appreciate everything they have taught you, all the love they have shown you, and how much you've grown in the relationship.

9) Thank them. If you are grateful for the affair, thank them for all that they have shared with you.

10) Share priorities. Tell them that you are working on your marriage and that your relationship with your spouse is now your priority.

After the Break-Up

Depending on your relationship with your spouse, and how transparent you've been about your affair, you might someday share with them the experience you've had of breaking up the affair. Your spouse may trust you even more if he or she understands how you ended it, and that you did so with integrity.

Simply telling your spouse that you sent your affair partner an email that stated, "I can never see you again," may not be sufficient proof that you are done. Your spouse may still doubt that the affair is completely over or believe that you're truly recommitting to the marriage. You may need to be more explicit and be prepared to work harder to demonstrate that you're taking responsibility for the consequences of your affair.

If you want to stay married to your spouse and make things work, sit down and talk about how each of you feel about how you ended the affair. If you show that you are ready to put all of your energy now into your marriage, your partner may believe that you are ready and able to create a new phase of your marriage and a sustainable monogamy.

Meanwhile there are still after-effects from ending your affair.

An Affair's After-Effects

1) Grief. You may have had a fantasy that the affair would work out better than it did. You now have to grieve the end of that fantasy.

2) Guilt and Remorse. The guilt and remorse over hurting your spouse may at times be intense. Bringing all of yourself back into your marriage may also be difficult. It may seem, at times, like you'll never be able to move forward.

3) Feelings. Take some time to let your feelings run the gamut—from hurt and confusion to regret and relief.

4) Confusion. You might regret ending the affair and want to contact your affair partner. Ambivalence is normal. Think carefully about their feelings before you reach out to them. One moment of contact or a phone call could mean months or years of emotional after effects.

Are there any other thoughts you have about what you might experience after ending an affair? They are probably all true and right and correct. Don't underestimate the impact of ending one relationship while you are still in your marriage. This can create a difficult, and sometimes quite complicated, emotional state.

Endnotes

xxxi Sept 2018, personal interview with Janis Spring author of After the Affair

xxxii http://www.yourtango.com/2016288524/study-says-being-cheated-good-you-bad-mistress?bt_email=tammy@tammynelson.org&bt_ts=1462385162690://www.oxfordhandbooks.com/view/10.1093/oxfordhb/9780199376377.001.0001/oxfordhb-9780199376377-e-19#oxfordhb-9780199376377-e-19-div1-8

CHAPTER EIGHT
Should I Stay or Should I Go?

It's time to take a hard look at your situation. Should you end your marriage? Or try to make it work? Either choice will affect your happiness, sexual well-being, material comfort, financial security and family life.

There are many reasons why you might find yourself struggling to arrive at a decision.

Here are a few things to consider. We're living longer than ever before—sometimes for as much as eighty, ninety or even one hundred years. If we've married young that means committing to one person for possibly seventy or eighty years—that's a long time to stay monogamous, particularly when so many relationships lack sexual excitement and are, let's face it, boring. Along with increasing longevity, there's the internet and social media, which have made it easier than ever to cheat with a myriad of partners.

Previous generations didn't have to wrestle with

these options: their lives were generally shorter. Only a few centuries ago, we lived to be an average of thirty-eight years old and were married for fifteen years. We can live with anyone for fifteen years. By the time we were bored with each other, we were dead. Back then, men and women stayed married to ensure their property would pass on to heirs. Or because marriage was the only option to have children, and avoid the penury of spinsterhood or the dependence on parents and family members. Two hundred years ago, men and women needed a spouse to help with the work of staying alive in very difficult times; with no conveniences, daily life was a series of grueling chores just to feed, stay clothed and keep warm. One couldn't go it alone; life was too tough.

Even one hundred years ago, people stayed married to have a regular sex life. There really wasn't a choice, particularly for women.

Today, marriage isn't a necessity for either sex. We don't need to marry to have children, or to buy property. We don't need to get married to get a mortgage or even life or health insurance, we can do all this without marrying. There's really no reason why people *need* to be married. Marriage and monogamy are a choice.

And so perhaps marriage is simply a holdover of an antiquated moral code.

Or maybe it's a desire to form mate bonds, to create meaningful dyads, and we continue to make promises to one another simply because, without these vows, we aren't sure we can really lead happy and personally fulfilling lives. We do it because we want to, not because we have to.

Many of us don't like to think of marriage as optional. We don't like to think that the structures that have forged our parents' lives and our grandparents' lives no longer have relevancy. That they might, in fact, be breaking down. We are determined, even driven, to keep at it. We try to make marriage, as we know it, work out, even in the face of evidence that it is not working. But we keep trying, we try to hold ourselves to the standard, rules and structures of monogamy that we have been using for over two hundred years.

And so, we continue to marry at the same time we're breaking our marital vows and promises. In diverse and underground ways, we're challenging these age-old structures, at an astonishingly high rate.

Marriage has been a centralizing moral force; a religious, cultural, and ethical guiding principal for hundreds of years. Whether you had two parents, or grew up in a single-parent home, marriage is still, as it has been, the guiding force of our society.

Yet, for you, the cheater, it's not working for you. Why?

Are You in Love?

Helen E. Fisher, author of *Why We Love: The Nature and Chemistry of Romantic Love,* [18]investigates and researches love. She studies the neurochemical pathways that regulate attachments to help understand why and how we form relationships.

In her lab she scanned the brains of people who were in love in by putting them in an fMRI (functional magnetic resonance imaging) machine and checking out the results. Dr. Fisher discovered that there are three distinct stages of love: the sexual drive stage, the romantic love stage, and the attachment stage.

Lust

The sexual drive, or lust, is driven by hormones, including testosterone and estrogen, which make us crave sex. Being in lust is similar to being on drugs—opiates in particular. The increase in serotonin, oxytocin and vasopressin—essentially endogenous opioids (the body's natural

---

18   Helen E. Fisher,(2004) *Why We Love: The Nature and Chemistry of Romantic Love,* Henry Holt, NY

equivalent of heroin)—makes us feel relaxation, pleasure and satiety. It also induces bonding.

Romance

The romantic love stage includes the symptoms of being "love-struck": loss of appetite, difficulty sleeping, inability to concentrate, and obsessive thinking about the other person. This "romantic" or "obsessive" phase is accompanied by the "butterflies in the stomach" feeling, which is due to a chemical reaction in the body. The norepinephrine and serotonin released during the romantic phase makes us feel jittery and excited, while dopamine gives us feelings of happiness and well-being. These "love chemicals" also include PEA, or phenylethylamine, the same substance found in chocolate and in strawberries. (This is why typical Valentine's Day gifts make total sense.)

According to Dr. Fisher, "People who jump from relationship to relationship crave the intoxication of falling in love and may be what she calls "attraction junkies." From her fMRI brain scans, Fisher found that "romantic love is a drive, an instinct that arises from primitive parts of the brain associated with dopamine, a powerful stimulant." Romance, it seems, is simply a chemical high.

Attachment

The attachment stage is a different type of love, a feeling of safety, a sense of security and calmness, a bond you believe you can have with that will last a long time, if not forever.

Dr. Fisher explains that you can feel all three things—lust, romantic love, and attachment—for the same person *or* for different people at the same time: "You can feel deep attachment for a long-term spouse, while you feel romantic love for someone else, while you feel the sex drive in situations unrelated to either partner." She says, "This independence means it is possible to love more than one person at a time, a situation that leads to jealousy, adultery, and divorce."

Should I Leave My Spouse for My Lover?

Does all of this mean that infidelity is purely a result of your brain function? It can be tough to decide what to do with these warring functions in your brain. You could be struggling with these questions: "Do I love my affair partner?" "Do I love my spouse, enough?" "Which one do I love more?" What if, as Helen Fisher suggests, you love them both, but in different ways?

If so, the bad news is this: if you leave your spouse for your lover, it's unlikely you'll end up living happily ever after.

It turns out, as mentioned earlier, that only a handful of cheaters end up with their lovers. Remember, only 3 percent of men marry the women they have affairs with, and the divorce rate is high (about 75 percent) among those who do marry their affair partners. It seems that having an affair does not, in fact, create lasting happiness.

What Does it Take to Stay with My Spouse?

Staying committed to one partner for many years isn't easy. Couples in long-term, committed relationships have to learn many difficult relationship skills, including frustration tolerance, self-control, patience, a conscious empathy and, perhaps the most important skill of all, kindness. But staying can mean more than just being nice to your spouse. It might mean you'll have to get over your relationship with your affair partner.

How Do I Get Over My Affair Partner?

You'll never be the same person as you were before the affair, and your marriage will never be the same relation-ship because of it.

Although this may be painful to hear, the good news is that you now have the opportunity to create a better, stronger, more vibrant relationship with your spouse—if you choose to end the affair and stay married. If you are both committed to working through the issues you had before the affair, it's possible to create a new, and, yes, a happy marriage.

Remember That Wake-Up Call?

What if you could have a whole new marriage or committed relationship with your current partner? Is it possible that despite the incredible pain the affair has created in your relationship, that the affair was just a wake-up call? Could you imagine a new type of relationship that might work better for the both of you?

It *is* possible to create a "new monogamy," a new relationship with your spouse in which both your needs and desires are explicitly stated and validated. You could have a new marriage, not just a revived old one—something altogether different, and with the spouse you have now.

With this new monogamy you can both create a relationship that works for you, regardless of the standard cultural norms or expectations, as long as the terms of your new relationship are explicitly stated and agreed upon by both of you.

Vital to this arrangement is communication. You need to take the opportunity to talk openly and honestly, and perhaps more bravely than you ever have about your needs in this new partnership.

Long-Term Relationship With Your Affair Partner?

You might feel broken-hearted at the idea of leaving your affair partner. If so, then you may not be ready to work on revitalizing your marriage. You might need time, or you might need therapy to get clear on what you want.

Things *Not* To Do at This Point

Don't lie and say the affair is over if it isn't.

Don't say you want to work on your marriage if you don't.

Don't give your affair partner hope or make false promises.

Don't ignore the situation hoping it will all smooth over with time.

Things *To Do* at This Point

Honor your own ambivalence.

Accept that what you want may not be an option.

Give yourself time to think.

Find a therapist if you need one.

Still confused? Try the exercise below to get clarity on whether your affair partner is the one for you.

Listening to Your Inner Voice

Sit down in a quiet place. Have a pad of paper or your journal and a pen close by. Make sure you're in a comfortable place (and shut your phone off).

1) Close your eyes and take a few deep breaths.

2) Feel the ground underneath you.

Do a scan of your body—from your feet to your head and back down.

Notice what your body feels like—which parts are stressed, tight, in pain.

Notice what else is happening in your body and let go of your thoughts

Scan your heart and mind for emotion; what are you feeling?

Where do you feel your emotion?

Notice the difference between your thoughts and your emotions.

Now imagine your affair partner. Picture them walking toward you.

See them clearly as they get closer to you. They are smiling.

Now scan your body again for emotions and thoughts. What are you feeling?

Notice what you feel, and notice any words or . thoughts that come to mind.

In your mind, thank your affair partner for all they have given you.

Say goodbye and watch them turn and walk away.

Notice your thoughts and your emotions as he/she walks off into the distance.

Ask yourself if you should stay in this relationship and for how long.

What are the thoughts and emotions you experience? Be honest.

Take a deep breath and thank yourself for doing this, and for being present.

Stretch and shake out your fingers and toes.

Pick up your journal and write down every detail you can remember.

For Your Journal

Reminder:

What I am experiencing …

What I feel in my body…

What I feel in my emotions…

Things that I see clearly…

What I hear…

What I know…

When Your Partner Knows

If your partner knows about the affair, the atmosphere at home may be uncomfortable—even difficult. You may hear things from your spouse like, "I don't even know you," or "What could that other person have seen in you?" Treat these as worthy conversational openers; as areas to explore in your marriage. You don't know what you don't know about one another.

Now might be the time for both of you to explore what you have been keeping from one another.

Can Your Partner Get Over It?

It's time to sit down and talk with your spouse about what you want. If you think you want to end your affair and stay together, you may want to renegotiate a "new monogamy" together, and talk about what it will take to make it work. If you each put new energy into this, you may find that you can both create a new marriage and a new, sustainable monogamy. But that's only if your spouse can talk about and integrate what you've done. They may want nothing to do with you. Or they may need time; or weeks or months of therapy, first without you and then with you. They may need a vacation just to get away and think.

And even then, it may not work out between you.

Recovery

There are three easily identifiable phases of recovery that happen after an affair: the crisis phase, the understanding (or insight) phase, and the vision phase. [xxxi]

I introduced Maddie and Bo, earlier. Maddie and Bo had been in therapy for a year, coming in for sessions together twice a month. They were still working on their marriage and both were dedicated to making things work between them. Maddie had cheated on Bo with four other men while she was away on business trips. Maddie had assumed that her affairs wouldn't matter to Bo since he had cheated in the past, and she knew that he also had a penchant for visiting strip clubs.

But immediately after Bo uncovered her infidelities, things between them blew up. When I first saw them for therapy, they were still in the crisis phase of their recovery. Bo was angry while Maddie sought to play down the importance of her affairs. During this time, Bo and Maddie weren't sure they would or could stay together.

The Phases of Recovery:
The Crisis Phase

The first phase of affair recovery, or the crisis phase,

happens as soon as an affair is disclosed or discovered. The initial shock and deep betrayal can rock the confidence of the betrayed partner, and make them feel like everything they've believed about the marriage is a lie. Perversely, for the cheater, the crisis phase may be an exciting time and intensify his or her attraction and romantic feelings for the affair partner. At the same time, they may be consumed by feelings of intense regret, guilt, and shame.

In the crisis phase emotions are high. For Bo and Mattie who were trying to reconcile, I reminded them that this was only a phase: "Eventually this time will pass, and you'll move into another stage."

They weren't ready to believe me. Bo wanted to leave. "I can't trust her, she lied, and now she's minimizing the affair."

Maddie, on the other hand, didn't think she could stay with Bo. "He's over-reacting, reading all my emails, going through my stuff. I can't live like this!"

I warned them both that making any decisions now, during a crisis, wouldn't be wise. "Don't decide now what to do with your relationship; don't make any long-term decisions about your marriage or even about your affair. Now is the time to take care of yourselves, and your family."

"But," Maddie said, "I want to leave; to take some time to be by myself."

I advised her that during the crisis she should hold off on making any major decisions, at least for a while. When the chaos in their relationship lessened, then they could start to think about whether or not they wanted to stay together or break up and move on. But, until that time, they needed to adjust their feelings to the new situation they both found themselves in.

Initially, after infidelity has been exposed, it's difficult for the cheater and the spouse and, yes, the affair partner, to envision any sort of future together.

For the spouse who's been cheated on, it can seem like there's no one to turn to. The person they previously relied on for comfort is now the betrayer.

The cheater may now view the marriage as a liability instead of an asset. It may seem more of an unpleasant burden than a sanctuary; no longer a partnership providing comfort and hope.

The affair partner—whether single or married—may feel put on hold, waiting and wondering what will happen and resentful that plans for a future together might now be dissipating. They may also worry about retaliation from the spouse, or abandonment by the cheater.

All three individuals entangled in the affair may feel lonely and confused.

As each player in the affair triangle grieves for the death of the relationship they once had, they'll also despair for any relationship going forward.

None of the players will grieve at the same rate, or perhaps even at the same time. Recovery, too, for all will occur at different rates. Imagine yourselves as trains moving at different speeds, never moving at the same time or on the same track.

If you are in the crisis phase after an affair, it's probably safe to assume that, before the affair, you couldn't imagine reaching the place you're in now—nor did your spouse. You're both grieving what you may think is the end of a life—a dream of a loving and monogamous relationship in which you would both grow old and retire. That dream and your hopes have been dashed.

As the cheater, you're probably well ahead of your spouse in the recovery process. You've known about the affair longer than they have, and been (subconsciously, perhaps) mentally preparing for this moment of crisis. Your spouse, however, is far behind you—they've only just discovered you've been having an affair, and are only beginning to grapple with the crisis. Not only are the two of you at different points in the healing process, your spouse may never catch up.

It isn't easy ending an affair. You may have thought this would all turn out differently than it did. Endings can be complicated and it can hurt to let go.

As you move through the process, you'll experience many intense emotions. Lots of feelings will emerge: for you, your spouse and your affair partner, including anger, fear, denial and, hopefully, acceptance.

Grieving clears the way for new possibilities. The first steps, though, require looking at yourself and taking the time to understand what happened so you can make your way through the next phases of healing.

The Understanding Phase

The second phase of affair recovery is the understanding (or insight) phase, and you'll know when you're entering this phase; it's when you start to reflect on how the affair came to be. This second phase of affair recovery comes once the crisis phase begins to ebb, and you're both moving past intense anger or confusion.

This can be a difficult time, but this phase can help both of you to experience empathy for the other and can give you hope. You may still not know whether you want to make things work but you will be able to do some of the work on the past, to find out how the affair(s) happened and why.

After several months of being in crisis, Bo and Mattie were in my office again. Bo began, "We had these affairs, and now we want to understand why we've been doing this to each other throughout our whole marriage. Why did we choose to marry someone who was not going to be faithful when we swore that's what we wanted in a marriage?"

Maddie expressed curiosity as to why Bo married her, "He knew I was never going to be monogamous. I told him when we first met that I had never been interested in monogamy and I'd never been faithful to one man, ever. I wanted an open marriage. Bo didn't. I reluctantly agreed to it when we got married, because he wanted it, but I wasn't happy. And now he acts all surprised! Surprised that I'm the same person he met all those years ago."

After hearing Maddie's complaint, Bo agreed. "It's true. I knew Maddie felt like this. I feel like, maybe, well, I believed, deep down, that I could change her. I thought that, for me, she would change. I thought that I could make her love me enough, to want only me."

"So," I asked Bo, after we had been doing many months of deep therapy work around his "family of origin" story, "were you trying to get Maddie to love you, in the way your mother never did?"

Bo started to tear up. "I guess I thought I could make her love me if I was good enough. Then when I cheated on her I guess I felt like I didn't deserve her love. So, I pushed her away and, of course, she had other relationships. It makes sense now that I think about it."

Understanding the cheating and how it could have happened and why will help you, and possibly your partner too, to be clear about what led you to this point in your life. This means that, as the cheater, you'll need to dig deep to get to the truth behind your actions, and why you began the affair.

During this second phase of affair recovery, you may wonder how much responsibility lies with your marriage partner (did their neglect or lack of desire lead you to start an affair, for instance?). But this phase shouldn't be about assigning blame, it's about deconstructing the affair to uncover the roots of your infidelity.

Journaling Exercise

Was there infidelity in my parent's marriage?

What did my parents teach me about monogamy?

Where did I learn about love?

What were my assumptions about my marriage?

Starting to understand the affair can answer many of the questions you may have about your behaviors and your marriage. Some of your frustration may make more sense, and you may be ready to make some decisions about the potential for a shared future with your spouse.

Moving Past Blame

If both partners are ready to move into healing, there'll be a noticeable shift. Instead of feeling polarized, and being pushed into the "good" spouse and "bad" spouse roles, the two of you will begin to see that you each share some responsibility for what happened in your relationship prior to the affair. There was most likely a dynamic in your marriage that contributed to the affair. Once you identify and acknowledge this dynamic, the recovery process becomes a shared experience between the two of you. The affair may even move from being "your affair" to being "our affair."

When you make this shift, it means you're moving through the understanding phase and you may be ready for the vision phase, where you begin to imagine a new relationship with a new type of shared monogamy agreement.

Perel[19] says, "…infidelity is less likely to be a symptom of a problem, and is more often described as an expansive experience that involves growth, exploration and transformation."

This phase of understanding can change everything. "Understanding why the infidelity happened and what it signified is critical, both for couples who choose to end their relationship and for those who want to stay together, rebuild and revitalize theirs."

The Vision Phase

When you reach the third phase of affair recovery, the vision phase, it's time to make some decisions about staying together or moving on to begin separate lives. In this phase, you can decide whether or not it's even possible to create a new future together after all the hurt between you. To do this, you should set aside a time to discuss the possibility of a new monogamy agreement.[xxxii]

The idea of a "new monogamy" challenges the common view that committed relationships can only mean intimacy between two primary partners, and that an affair has to mean the end of a relationship. Monogamy, in our

---

19   Perel, Esther (2018) State of Affairs, Harper Collins, NY

Western culture, is becoming more nuanced. Couples who manage to re-invent their relationships after infidelity can be more creative, open-minded and flexible in their partnerships, and may even find ways to make their brand of "monogamy" work for them.

Bo and Maddie ultimately decided that, if they were going to stay together, they had many things to discuss; and many things they would need to agree on—including what could happen during Maddie's business trips and whether Bo's strip club visits would be off-limits, or not. They would need to discuss the erotic side of their relationship, too. How often would they have sex? What if it wasn't satisfying? How would they even broach these topics?

A new monogamy agreement is something that the two of you have to agree on, and it doesn't have to be the same as your original agreement, in fact it shouldn't be. It should be flexible—an agreement that can be modified as you continue to work on your marriage. The important thing is to have an ongoing discussion about how you want things to be between you.

Try not to listen to your well-meaning family and friends. They might say you're crazy for staying together. But they're not in your marriage. They don't know your history or your feelings for each other. It's easy for outsiders to pass judgment. Don't let anyone shame you into believing you've made a mistake by staying in your marriage. This new relationship is between the two of you, only.

Erotic Recovery

The next step toward moving past an affair, and making your relationship work, is moving toward a new intimacy and connection.

"Erotic recovery" is working on the part of your relationship that is purely sexual. An affair is like an injury to that part of your marriage. In order to heal, you have to heal the erotic part. What should you do first? You will need to actually sit down and discuss your sexual relationship.

Start by Asking

Here are some basic questions to ask to begin on the journey to erotic recovery:

How often will we have sex now that we are working on our committed future?

What kind of sex are we interested in having?

How will we make this discussion easy for both of us?

What type of reminders will we use to keep our sex

life vital and alive?

Frankly, in any relationship you have, whether it's with your spouse, your affair partner or someone new, you'll want to focus on enhancing your erotic life through open dialogue about your expectations. Having a healthy sex life will guarantee passion and more "aliveness" for both of you.

Getting the Intimacy You Want

Use the following questions to create an open dialogue with your partner:

When do you feel the most intimate with me?

What makes you feel loved and adored?

What do you find sexy about me?

If we have a great sex life, what will it look like? (Be specific)

What can we do tonight to improve our sex life?

What should we do over the next week/month/year to make things sexier?

Have an Affair With Your Spouse

You want to be more than just roommates. To accomplish this, you'll need to put effort into making your sex life exciting. Remember, your affair partner was the "ideal" sex partner. If you had stayed together, it's likely that time and familiarity would have taken their toll on your "perfect" sex life and you would have had to work at it to keep it satisfying, just like you're going to have to do now. *Good sex takes commitment.* Are you ready to commit to making your sex life the best it can be?

If so, do you want sex with your spouse to feel dangerous, naughty, illicit and forbidden? As good as your affair sex?

Start with some frank discussions with your spouse about what you really want in bed. Use the Erotic Recovery Dialogue prompts below to talk about your fantasies; about what really turns you on. It's time to be honest about what you really desire.

The Erotic Recovery Dialogue works. I've been using this to help guide my clients for more than twenty years. The dialogue always stirs up excitement. (And, to be honest, I do it with my partner too—a lot. And it works for us; in fact, I wouldn't suggest it if I hadn't had success with it.)

To begin, find a comfortable place to sit or lay down together. Take a few minutes for some deep breathing. Stay committed to the purpose of this conversation. Hold the space for your partner by simply "mirroring" everything they say.

Always start with an appreciation of your partner

to decrease any nervousness or defensive feelings. Mirroring the appreciation sounds something like this: Your partner says, "I really appreciate that you are such a good listener," and you simply mirror, or repeat back, "So, you really appreciate that I am a good listener."

If you are the *Receiver*, you don't have to thank the *Sender*, or apologize or make excuses or agree or disagree. Just listen. And mirror. Then switch roles and your partner mirrors your comments.

Erotic Recovery Dialogue

1) One thing I appreciate about you:
2) One thing I appreciate about our intimate life:
3) One thing I like about our sex life that I want more of:
4) One thing I have never tried that I would like to:
5) One thing I appreciate about being able to talk to you about this:

Switch being the *Sender* and be the *Receiver*.

Role-Playing

"Ninety-eight percent of men and seventy-eight percent of women have fantasized about someone other than their

spouse."[20]

One of the easiest ways to bring back the spark is to role-play. This can take some practice, and will require effort, but it may give both of you the chance to get back to how you were with each other when you first met. Put aside your current role of husband or wife or partner and embrace a new persona. Acting out your fantasies can be just as exciting (and maybe more exciting) as having an affair. I know many couples who've role-played and "met as strangers" in a bar with the result that their "married affair" becomes a torrid one.

Maddie and Bo were focused on their erotic recovery. They made a date to try some role-play. Maddie waited for Bo at his favorite strip club. As much as she resented him for his taste in bars, she found it exciting to walk in alone and sit at the bar alone. She watched the girls on stage who danced around the poles and found herself interested if a little distant. She ordered a drink. Out of the corner of her eye she saw Bo walk in. He

---

20   Druckerman, Pamela 2008 Lust in Translation: Infidelity from Tokyo to Tennessee Penguin Books NY

looked around and noticed her at the bar. When he sat down next to her and offered to buy her a drink, he asked her "What's your name?" They both smiled. "This is fun," Maddie thought.

When they talked about the night in therapy, Maddie said she liked feeling like a stranger, not only to Bo, but to herself. "I was able to explore a part of myself I didn't even know I had in me."

"And I loved that stranger, the stranger in her!" Bo said.

If you can be open with your partner about what you want, and how you're going to get it, your "married sex" can be just as hot as affair sex, without any of the risk. Let your partner know who you really are, what you really want, what you truly desire.

What will happen if you don't try something new? If you refuse to work on your erotic life? Will it get better on its own?

What if You Decide to End Your Marriage?

You may decide, during the vision stage, that it's time to end your marriage. The affair may be the tip of a massive iceberg that's been lurking beneath your seemingly placid—or perhaps tumultuous—co-existence for some time. Or maybe it's your partner who sees the affair as a way of getting out of what has been, for them, an unhappy relationship.

So, the decision has been made: the marriage is done. But, even so, don't be quick to rewrite the history of your relationship. Although you may be thankful it's ending during this time of turmoil, you need to recognize that there were probably lots of happy times, and good memories between you.

"The opposite of death is desire…" —**Tennessee Williams**

Am I a Failure at Marriage?

We love to be in love and we hate breaking up. Ending a relationship feels like failure. If our marriage ends, most of us will feel as if we've failed. Against the best advice, once we've decided to divorce, we all try and rewrite the experience of our entire marriage, deriding ourselves and our lack of judgment for marrying the "wrong" person.

Most of us aren't good at navigating divorce. In America, divorce is a multi-billion-dollar business, one that enriches lawyers and impoverishes couples, ratcheting up our anger and contentiousness. Bitter divorces harm our children and rip apart families, including in-laws, ex-laws and friends. There's seemingly nothing good about divorce—not unless we can take the time to do it consciously and with well-thought-out intention, respect, and compassion.

Most of us have bought into the Romeo-and-Juliet ideal of having one life partner—the fantasy of finding our soul mate. So, when the marriage with our "soul mate" ends, we convince ourselves that we chose wrong, that this person in the end wasn't our true soul mate, and that now we'll trade our first spouse in for a better model—the affair partner, or someone else who's still out there, somewhere.

Perhaps this model of romance is not all there is to love. Maybe in this time of longer lives, healthier standards of sexuality and back-to-back monogamy, maybe we can have multiple relationships. Maybe we just need to be better at divorce.

Intentional Divorce

Maybe being intentional at divorcing, being kinder, more respectful, could eliminate some of the pain of our in-between times.[21]   Intentional divorce is a concept, a

21   Nelson, Tammy, (2015) The Intentional Divorce: Helping Couples Let Go With Dignity
Psychotherapy Networker Magazine: Psychotherapy Networker
Vol/Issue:Vol. 39, No. 4, July/August 2015

new way of looking at this transitional time, the time that for many people is inevitable after an affair or a painful breakup. But a divorce doesn't have to be a time of devastation, a financial roadblock or a destroyer of families.

Today, intentional divorce can be a more contemporary, and a more humane model of divorce. No one is more determined to help couples successfully move through a more civil and respectful process of "conscious uncoupling" than Katherine Woodward-Thomas, author of *Conscious Uncoupling: 5 Steps To Living Happily Even After*. Thomas has helped thousands of couples find caring ways to bring marriages to an end, without creating needless pain. In her conscious uncoupling work, couples can split apart with minimal damage, and even promote healing to one another and to their families.

Thomas says there are five steps to get through a breakup and still "live happily after."

Find Emotional Freedom

Reclaim Your Power and Your Life

Break the Pattern

Become a Love Alchemist:

Create Your Happily-Even-After Life

This more "Conscious Uncoupling" process makes divorce easier to deal with and maybe even a growth opportunity for both partners. If you are interested in

finding out more about Conscious Uncoupling, go to
www.consciousuncoupling.com.

It's a Completion, Not an Ending

> *"That it will never come again*
> *is what makes life sweet."*
>
> -Emily Dickinson

What if our traditional model of love – the romantic idealistic narrative of "everyone has *one* soul mate" model of relationship no longer applied? What if the story of love went like this – we meet someone wonderful, fall in love, marry them and learn all we can from each other, and then, eventually, perhaps, inevitably, we came to the end of that relationship? What if we could "complete" our marriages instead of ending them? What if we accomplished all we could with our love mate and then, feeling complete, we became ready to move on? What if we learned to say thank you to one another for all we had learned, for the times we had spent together, to truly appreciate the relationship we had, and then, eventually, when we were ready, we could leave with respect and collaboration and move on to find a new mate who had other things to teach us?

If this new model of love were accepted, if we all felt that this was the "norm," if most, if not all of our love stories included a respectful ending, an intentional goodbye, as part of our loving narrative, if transitions were done well, would we approach divorce in ways that were less destructive? Might we act with more kindness, respect, and appreciation when our marriages and relationships ended?

What if we used a mediator instead of a divorce lawyer and recognized that, to raise a happy and healthy child, we'd need to work together after divorce, as co-parents, with a co-parenting life-long agreement, to continue taking care of our children? And what if this agreement included all of our new spouses, as well as our exes?

What if we had multiple caring relationships throughout our lifetimes; what if we switched partners like we switched jobs, always moving up, and moving on after we'd learned all we could; not burning our bridges but appreciating each experience, each person - *as if each partner we met were our soul mate?*

What if we acknowledged that we could have many soul mates, and that everyone we fell in love with was meant to be in our lives?

What if we could do this with several soul mates, all at the same time?

229

Endnotes

xxxi Nelson, Tammy (2012) The New Monogamy; Redefining your relation-
     ship After Infidelity, New Harbinger Press, Oakland CA

xxxii Nelson, Tammy

CHAPTER NINE:
Creating A New Vision

Visioning

Think seriously about what you want. Maybe you've tried to make things work. You gave up your lover. You broke off your affair. You closed your online profile. You've done the dialogue, you had the talks, you've created a new monogamy agreement. And you're still not happy.

If that's the case, it's time to get serious about your vision for the future. What do you really want? What do you think will make you happy? What do you imagine will lead you to a wonderful life, the one you've been fantasizing about?

Can you imagine yourself leaving, being alone, being with someone new, starting over? Take some time to think, imagine and visualize. Give yourself enough time and space to answer the more pressing questions about your future.

Take out a journal or pad of paper. Write down the answers to the following questions.

What is My Vision for the Future?

Even though you may not be thinking about these things constantly, they are most likely on your mind. It helps to get these thoughts out and down on paper, or at least talk about them. And when you can talk about them with a partner, you can create a future, the future that you have always desired. Think for a moment about some of your fears and worries, but then also consider what you really desire for your future. Can you share these thoughts about your own personal dreams but also you vision for you and your partner?

The following is a way to journal about your vision. Write down your answer to these questions and then use your answers to talk to your partner about your new future.

-What is my vision for us as a couple?
-What are my fears?
-What are my worries?
-What are my desires?

What do I really want?
-What are my fears?
-What are my worries?
-What are my desires?

Are you clearer now about what you want? Can you make some changes now with your current partner? What things can you change? *Will* you change?

Michele Weiner- Davis, author of *Divorce Busting, A Step by Step Approach*, says to focus on what's working, not what's not. "When something troubling in a marriage happens, the spouse most bothered by the problem tries to fix it. If that doesn't work, the fixer escalates his or her efforts or does more of the same."[12] She says instead, "notice what's different about a time the problem situation occurs but didn't bother you."

For instance, if you worry that your partner will ignore your needs, can you instead identify a time when your needs were not met, but instead of it bothering you, you were in fact, relieved that you had time to yourself, or that you were able to meet your partner's needs, and that was satisfying in itself?

Changing your own behavior, noticing when things work instead of when things don't, and focusing on what you can change instead of how you might change your partner, can all lead to a new kind of relationship

---

12   Weiner-Davis, Michele, (1993) Divorce Busting; A step by step Approach, A Fireside Book, NY

in your life. These changes take a kind of insight and self-awareness that come from examining your motivations, your thinking about your past behaviors and what you want going forward.

Are you like Gigi—do you want to cheat to stay in your marriage? Are you like Bo and Maddie, who both cheated but who ultimately stayed together? Or are you like Ramesh—do you want to end things to try and make your affair partner a more permanent relationship partner?

If you choose any of these options, you are going to have to consider some important things.

Michele Weiner-Davis, Author of *Healing from Infidelity*, said "If you want to save your marriage, no matter how justified you might feel about the reasons you strayed, regardless of the problems in your marriage or the seeming unreasonableness of your spouse's current demands, you must assume the lion's share of the responsibility for healing your partner's pain. Humility, contrition, patience and a willingness to do whatever it takes to rebuild trust is what it will require."

Micro-Cheating

"Self-discipline is self-caring."
— M. Scott Peck, The Road Less Traveled

Now that you've decided to make some changes in your life, stick to your vision. Keep yourself in check. Watch what you do. Be responsible. Don't let yourself sink into denial. It's easy for micro-cheating behavior traits to sneak up on you. You may be in the midst of another cycle of cheating or pre-cheating behavior and not even recognize that you are starting things up again, either with your old affair partner or with someone new. Micro-cheating includes behavior such as flirting online, or sending sexy emails or texts. Or talking extensively on the phone to someone other than your partner.

Micro-cheating can include things like sending photos of yourself to friends or strangers online, or even direct-messaging jokes or memes on social media. Micro-cheating can be anything that crosses that line—the line that you know you shouldn't cross if you want to stay monogamous. How do you know where that line is? Consider it any behavior that you wouldn't want your partner to know about.

Microcheating sneaks up on you. Perhaps this has happened to you. You're only going out for drinks, or for lunch, or for an occasional "business" dinner, with a friend or colleague. You've had a few of these get-togethers.

This kind of casual relationship begins to turn into something more. You find yourself attracted to this person, you enjoy their company, you want to spend more time together. You text after dinner to say thanks. You send a snappy meme. Then they send you a selfie.

You avoid telling your wife or husband about the drinks, and then you lie about the dinners, blaming the late nights on business. Communication between you and this "casual friend" escalates, and you seek more opportunities to be with your "friend." You convince yourself there's nothing going on. Then, before you realize it, you are in a relationship.

Quite often it's the secret-keeping itself that turns the relationship from a friendship into an affair. Lying to cover up the meetings that up until then had been casual turn your get-togethers into something more, giving them meaning and a new energy. From then it's only a matter of time before the drinks and dinners become sexual liaisons. The casual dating affair transforms into a sexual affair, and then you're in too deep to stop.

If you find yourself justifying this behavior as "not really" breaking your monogamy agreement, think hard about what you *are* doing. If you wouldn't want your partner peering over your shoulder while you're doing it, then what you're doing might, in fact, be cheating.

Getting Therapy

Not surprisingly, couple therapists have reported extra-marital affairs to be one of the most damaging problems couples face, and one of the most difficult problems to treat.[xxxv] Yet it's the couples who choose to go into therapy who most often survive as a couple.

Therapy is a decision – a decision to choose love. Therapy can help couples who *want* their relationship to work. M. Scott Peck, a psychiatrist and the bestselling author of *The Road Less Traveled*,[xxxvi] wrote, "True love is not a feeling by which we are overwhelmed. It is a committed, thoughtful decision." He believed that for love to be successful it should be a conscious choice, not an overwhelming emotion that we have no personal control over. He believed that the purpose of a loving relationship is to support one another's growth. Can you see yourself choosing to be in a relationship that supports your partner's growth, one where you choose love?

The Evolved Marriage

"Twenty percent of single adults have practiced consensual non-monogamy at some point in their lives."

— Wednesday Martin, Author of *UNTRUE*

Marriage is evolving, adapting to our 21st-century sensibilities. You could have your cake and eat it too. And why shouldn't you? Most people, if they could arrange it, would want the cake and the marriage, too. But could you have it if you discussed it openly and instead of non-consensual non-monogamy you created a consensual non-monogamy agreement?

Twenty percent of all adults have practiced some form of consensual non-monogamy at some point in their adult lives.[13] More people than ever claim to be in open relationships—partnerships in which each person has the freedom to be with other people, both sexually and emotionally, depending on the agreement of both partners. How they manage their outside relationships and the time they spend together is up to them.

---

13   Martin, Wednesday, 2018, Untrue: Why Nearly Everything We Believe About Women, Lust, and Infidelity Is Wrong and How the New Science Can Set Us Free, Little, Brown Spark, NY, NY

Polyamory (*poly* meaning *many* and *amory* meaning *love)* is a lifestyle that more and more people are choosing as a result of the many challenges of marriage today. Polyamory is a multi-dimensional, consensually non-monogamous relationship in which each partner has many loving "outside" relationships while still maintaining the commitment and connection of the "inside" primary partnership.

Polyamorous couples (two people) and thruples (three people) and pods (more than three) recognize that they can each love many people, while still honoring the relationship(s). The connecting force is honesty and transparency, and the integrity of their flexible monogamy (or consensual non-monogamy) agreement is what keeps them together. This is a new kind of marriage, one in which couples make their own rules about what monogamy looks like.

A study in 2017, the first large-scale study on the prevalence of consensual non-monogamy[xxxvii] found that more than one in five Americans (about 21 percent) have engaged in the practice at some point in their lifetime. These findings suggest that open marriage is much more common than most people think. A study from three years earlier, in 2014, estimated the rate to be at only 5.3 percent.

How would you even begin to have the conversation about opening your relationship?

How to Have a Dialogue to Open Your Relationship

Could you and your partner have an open relationship? Or a polyamorous relationship? Try this dialogue. Remember to take turns being the *Sender* and the *Receiver*. When you are the *Receiver*, mirror everything that your partner is saying. And then switch.

Open Relationship Dialogue

Here's what I appreciate about our relationship now.

Here's one reason why I might appreciate an open relationship.

Can you think of one way that it might work for you?

How might it not work?

Here's one thing I could do to make it successful, if we tried.

One fear I have about opening our relationship is…

Here's one way I think it may help us.

Here's one reason I appreciate that we're having

this discussion.

When you are each finished listening and mirroring try empathizing and validating each other.

Validating sounds like "Knowing you the way I know you, it makes sense that…." Take turns validating each other's experience.

John and Aaron had a conversation in my office. John told Aaron, "Look, I don't want you to leave your husband; he loves you. But if you are feeling guilty, ask him to have an open relationship. Just don't drag me into the conversation. Frankly, if you leave him, I am not really into being your new husband, and I don't want you to blame me for ruining your marriage. But I understand if you want to change your monogamy agreement with him. That's between the two of you."

Aaron thought about it for a while and finally decided to go home and talk to his husband. He used the Open Relationship Dialogue.

When he came back to therapy with John, he described what happened. "So I asked my husband what was one way an open marriage might work for him. I was surprised that he said it might let him off the hook, sexually, since he knew I wanted more than he could give me. We had a much longer conversation about how he would feel if I had relationships with other men. And I talked for a long time about what it would be like for me if he was with other men. He said he's not really into that, but we had to have an important conversation about all of these things. Thank goodness we had the dialogue written down between us on a piece of paper, and kept going back to those sentence stems, it helped to have the structure to talk about this stuff. We were both nervous."

John said, "I hope you are not opening your marriage because of me."

Aaron said, "No, I really believe that this is the best thing for me right now. I love him and I don't want to leave him. We have a good thing going, please don't be hurt when I say that."

John looked at Aaron, "No, Aaron, truly, I am not hurt. I don't want you to leave your husband, please, work it out if you can. I don't want our relationship to end, you and me, but I also know that you love him too."

"Well, the good news is my husband said that if we kept the lines of communication open and if I still loved him and don't keep secrets, he said he was ok with it. Even, well, good with it."

Empathy

I explained to Aaron that after the sentence stems of the Dialogue, the idea is to try empathizing with each other's feelings. Saying things like, "It makes sense that you feel…" can help the Sender feel heard and understood.

"I was able to do that for my husband. I said 'I wonder if you are feeling afraid, or excited, and he actually said he was feeling both of those things, and he appreciated that I got where he was coming from."

Guessing at some feeling words that your partner may be experiencing as a result of the things you share can be helpful to the dialogue. You don't have to get them right all the time, it is more important that you try to connect with some feeling words to let your partner know you are trying to empathize and connect.

When You Get It

Whether you have an open marriage or polyamory or some version of a traditional monogamous marriage, an erotically satisfying marriage will most likely be the relationship that will keep you and your partner interested in one another and in your future.

Stephen Snyder, in his book, *Love Worth Making*,

[14]writes that sex has at least three ingredients. Pleasure and attraction are the more obvious ones. Sex therapists commonly refer to them as "friction plus fantasy." But sexual happiness in a committed relationship tends to require something more. "Somewhere beyond friction plus fantasy," he writes, "is a realm where sexuality connects us to each other and to the deepest parts of ourselves… Unlike friction and fantasy, this part of sex can't be bought, sold, marketed, or packaged as a commodity. It is simply a gift to be received. Its proper accompanying emotion is not really desire, or lust—but rather simply gratitude, or perhaps awe."

The Future of Affairs

Right now, in the United States and in the U.K., marriage rates are at their lowest point since 1895. And of those who are married, only 38 percent describe themselves as happy. What is even more intriguing, or troubling, is that 40 percent—over one-third—think that the institution of marriage is obsolete and that it simply just doesn't work. And so, what lies ahead for marriage?

We know that tech companies are now experimenting with robot partners: realistic robots with "brains" that

---

14   Snyder, Stephen (2018) Love Worth Making, NY

can remember our personal preferences, and memorize our calendars and our email. They can be programmed to have sex with us in the way we like, and then shut down and be put aside when we're done with them. Oh, and they'll never, ever argue or complain.

Is this the perfect spouse, or affair partner? Or, if we have a robot on the side, is having sex with a robot cheating?

What does the future of sex and technology mean for the future of marriage and monogamy? Perhaps every couple, every partner, every person, will have to make their own decision about what affairs, monogamy, marriage—and commitment of any kind—will look like as we move into the new realm of technological relationships that grow beyond what we are even able to imagine.

Relationships happen. They can happen between you and a partner, any partner—human or otherwise. And you can be anyone you decide to be in these relationships. Who will you decide to be?

Endnotes

xxxv Geiss & O'Leary, 1981; Whisman, Dixon, & Johnson, 1997.

xxxvi Peck, M. Scott, The Road Less Traveled

xxxvii Haupert ML, Gesselman AN, Moors AC, Fisher HE, Garcia JR, (2017) Prevalence of Experiences With Consensual Nonmonogamous Relationships: Findings From Two National Samples of Single Americans, J Sex Marital Ther. 2017 Jul 4;43(5):424-440.

CHAPTER TEN
Can You Have It All?

Cheating happens. Marriage, affairs, and sex are interwoven, and this meshing of intimacy and relationships may even create a form of altered but longer-lasting monogamy. We are in a time where partners everywhere are challenging the ideas and tenets of traditional "monogamy," examining some of the more antiquated ideas of how to make marriage work. Today we are forming new paradigms, new ideas and theories that put forth a more contemporary model of marriage and commitment.

Having Both

George is married. He lives in Minnesota. He's been married, for almost ten years. Sex is nonexistent, about three times a year. George has been cheating for about nine years. He has been quite successful at it. He has never been caught.

He works in technology and he has young children. When I asked him on the phone about his life and his marriage, he said he loves his kids, and his wife, but that her sex drive is low and he grew tired of asking her for sex. He said, "I am fine with her, she is great, I love her, she is a good mom, but I could only ask her so many times for sex without feeling rejected. And so, I found that cheating is a way to stay in my marriage without leaving her."

George asked his wife for couple's therapy and his wife refused. He asked her to go to a gynecologist for hormone treatment, but she refused. And so, George went onto Ashley Madison and onto Tinder, websites where he could seek dates with women who were single or married.

When he met the first woman for an extramarital affair, he felt like a weight had been lifted off of his shoulders. He kept the relationship compartmentalized, hidden from his wife. He said, "I didn't feel guilty. I felt like I had a couple of options. Option 1, I could get divorced, which I didn't want; Option 2, I could fix things in our relationship; or Option 3, I could cheat, which I need for sex and for human contact. I chose Option 3."

It seemed that George felt he had tried to fix things in is relationship and he didn't want to get divorced. He cared about his wife and loved his family.

"Over the past nine years, I have had sixteen lovers. The longest I have been with one person has been two years," George said. "Initially I felt like, ok, I still have it, I can meet women, this feels good, and then I settled down. And then longer term, I realized I don't need an exclusive lover. I am having sex now with partners that I like, I don't continue with them just to keep up appearances. I end things if I'm not happy."

I asked him how it felt to be online looking for lovers all the time. "Online it's hard. I have to talk a lot, I have to meet up to four people and communicate a lot to find someone. I go out a lot. I don't go in just wanting sex. It's not really what I want. It's just that I want to be satisfied. And they have to have an equal amount to lose.

"If I caught my wife cheating," George said, "I would accept it but I would be angry that she didn't tell me when I asked her, and I would accept an open marriage."

I asked George how he feels about his wife's sexual needs. He said, "I suspect my wife has physical hormonal issues and what is happening with her body is menopause, but every time I try to broach the subject she gets agitated."

Affairs are not easy. Not for the cheater. Yes, they can feel like an answer. They can feel like a solution. They can feel like, for the cheater, a way to have it all.

But George had advice for other cheaters, "When you can't cope with the guilt, or if you don't feel it, or if you are causing harm, then don't do it. Don't cause harm. If it's a plus, go ahead, if it's a minus for any reason then don't. Tell yourself that the reasons you are cheating are just as valid as the reasons you are in your marriage."

A Personal Message from the Author

Before I shut down my experiment on my personal Ashley Madison accounts, I took a last look at the account where I posed as Tom, and the account where I posed as Tina. Both accounts continue to receive messages from members looking for an affair, even though I had yet to respond to anyone. I have to be honest, as I read the requests, looked at the photos, and thought about it for more than a hot second, I did contemplate reaching out to a few of the members. Many of the emails were intriguing. Lots of the questions were interesting. It was nice to have both men and women be curious about me, about who I was and what I wanted in a relationship. I thought about it long and hard before I shut off the accounts and declined a more in-depth membership.

I thought about my current marriage and wondered what would happen if I were to pursue an affair. I trusted that the folks I would meet online would be discreet and I knew that if I didn't want to be caught, I wouldn't. I believe I could keep an affair a secret. There are obviously people out there who are interested.

And so, it seems that pursuing an affair is not that difficult. With online websites and opportunities everywhere, and because of the freedom and the access to explore nonconsensual nonmonogamy, I believe I, like many of you, could find a way to cheat if I wanted to.

And yet, for me, it's also a huge time-management issue. I personally find I can barely fit in time to spend with my own spouse, and I struggle to think how I might find the time for a lover on the side. But if I did want more excitement, more thrill, and a taste more of the kind of attention that I sense from my online pursuers, my first option would most likely be to create an expanded version of my monogamy agreement, a more open and flexible relationship with my husband. The transparency, for me, is a turn-on. Talking about what it might be like, what we could try, how we would do it, and who would want to do what if we were to open our marriage, is a thrilling idea. This kind of conversation is exciting because it pushes the boundaries of what is traditionally acceptable to even discuss in a marriage. It is even more exciting (and more practical) than trying to manage the secrecy of an affair. But that's just me. I know I could talk to my husband about the monogamy agreement we have and I could change it up if I had to. I am not sure how he would feel about it, or what he would say. But I would honor his feelings. If he didn't want to open the relationship and I was still invested in seeking out other partners, I might reconsider an extramarital relationship. I know now there are always options.

So, for today, I believe that talking and communicating about my current relationship with my husband is the first, the second, and the last step in what I hope is a long, sexy and exciting life for both of us.

I'll keep you posted.

The Future of the New Monogamy

The new monogamy offers hope for partnerships that are, if not ideal, at least (possibly) quite sustainable.

Divorce rates don't portend the death of marriage. We continue to marry, even after several divorces. People will always want to pair bond, even when they fail at it over and over again.

Maybe if we continue to approach our relationships in a fresh way, we can avoid inflicting deep, emotional wounds on each other and ourselves, and to the ones we love. Perhaps affairs provide clues about how to love; about what we need.

Regardless of your personal views on the established convention of marriage, of monogamy, you are someone who deserves an intimate, connected, and passionate relationship. Keep trying. Don't give up. Don't give up on love, on partnering, keep dreaming—of a future where you can find true happiness. You can create a happy, sustainable relationship.

THE END

"Sometimes the sins you haven't committed are all you have left to hold onto."

- David Sedaris

Dr. Tammy Nelson is the bestselling author of The New Monogamy, as well as Getting the Sex You Want. She is an internationally acclaimed sex and couples' therapist, a TED speaker and the host of a popular podcast. She lives and practices in the New York City area.

You can find her at www.drtammynelson.com, at www.whenyouretheonewhocheats.com, and on Twitter @drtammynelson.

REFERENCES

i   Atkins, Baucom, & Jacobson, 2001; Lauman, Gagnon, Michael, & Michaels, 1994

ii   Martin, Wednesday, 2018, Untrue: Why Nearly Everything We Believe About Women, Lust, and Infidelity Is Wrong and How the New Science Can Set Us Free, Little, Brown Spark, NY, NY

iii Drukerman, Pamela, 2008 in *Lust in Translation: Infidelity from Tokyo to Tennessee* Penguin Books; Reprint edition

iv Drukerman, *Lust in Translation: Infidelity from Tokyo to Tennessee*

v   Vaughan, Peggy, 2009, *The Monogamy Myth,* Newmarket Press; Third Edition, Harper Collins Publishers, NY, NY

vi Brown, Emily 2013 Patterns of Infidelity and Their Treatment, Routledge, 2nd edition

vii Spring, Janis, After the Affair,

viii Ashley Madison (AshleyMadison.com) data reveals that women have more sex after joining– (July 7, 2018) - Ashley Madison, the world's leading married dating website, surveyed its members to find out if their sexual personality traits differ between partners, and what kinds of sexual behavior they bring into the bedroom - Survey of 2,767 members of Ashley Madison between June 19, 2018, and July 5, 2018.

ix SURVEY reference

x   https://www.ncbi.nlm.nih.gov/pubmed/21152404

xi 2014 study https://www2.psy.uq.edu.au/~uqbziets/Zietsch et al 2014 Genetic analysis of extrapair mating.pdf

xii Hastings, Nick, Carter, Sue, Harbaugh, Caroll, Winslow, James, A role for central vasopressin in pair bonding in monogamous prairie voles, Nature volume 365, pages 545–548 (07 October 1993)

xiii Martin, Wednesday (2018) *Untrue: Why Nearly Everything We Believe About Women, Lust, and Infidelity Is Wrong and How the New Science Can Set Us Free, Harper Collins, NY NY*

xiv 2014 study https://www2.psy.uq.edu.au/~uqbziets/Zietsch percent20et percent20al percent202014 percent20Genetic percent20analysis percent20of percent20extrapair percent20mating.pdf

xv https://www.psychologytoday.com/us/blog/in-the-name-love/200811/pro-claimed-monogamy-clandestine-adultery

xvi Ben-Zeev, Aaron, (2004) Love Online, Emotions on the Internet, Cambridge University Press

xvii Perel, Esther (2018) State of Affairs, Harper Collins, NY, NY

xviii Diamond, Lisa (2009) Sexual Fluidity, Harvard University Press, Boston MA

xix https://www.menshealth.com/sex-women/a23301786/wednesday-martin-untrue/

xx https://www.fromgirltogirl.com/new-study-55-say-emotional-bond-is-cheating-ashley-madison/

xxi https://www.fromgirltogirl.com/new-study-55-say-emotional-bond-is-cheating-ashley-madison/

xxii Shaul Shalvi, Ori Eldar, Yoella Bereby-Meyer Honesty Requires Time (and Lack of Justifications) SAGE Journals First Published September 12, 2012 Research Article

xxiii Glass, Shirley, (2004) *Not Just Friends,* Emotional Affairs, Atria Books

xxiv *REF: This quiz by Shirley P. Glass was first printed in USA Today (June 20, 1988) in an article by Karen Peterson, "When platonic relationships get too close for comfort," p. 6D. Taken from the book NOT "Just Friends", ©2018 Dr. Shirley Glass

xxv *Journal of Marital and Family Therapy* (Vol. 34, No. 4) 2008 Hertlein

xxvi Spring, Janis, (2018) After the Affair, Harper Collins Publisher, rereleased 2018

xxvii Martin, Wednesday, 2018, *UNTRUE: Why Nearly Everything We Believe About Women, Lust, and Adultery is Wrong and How the New Science Can Set Us Free*

xxviii https://www.statisticbrain.com/infidelity-statistics/] [https://www.apa.org/pubs/journals/features/cfp-0000012.pdf][Couple and Family Psychology: Research and Practice © 2014 American Psychological Association 2014, Vol. 3, No. 1, 1–12 2160-4096/14/$12.00 DOI: 10.1037/cfp0000012 Infidelity and Behavioral Couple Therapy: Relationship Outcomes Over 5 Years Following Therapy Rebeca A. Marín Andrew Christensen University of Washington University of California Los Angeles David C. Atkins University of Washington

xxix Bahadur Rory Individual Sovereignty, Freer Sex, And Diminished Privacy: How An Informed And Realistic Modern Sexual Morality Provides Salvation From Unjustified Shame Elon.Edu (https://www.elon.edu/e/CmsFile/GetFile?FileID=551)

xxx Spring, Janis

xxxi Sept 2018, personal interview with Janis Spring author of After the Affair

xxxii http://www.yourtango.com/2016288524/study-says-being-cheated-good-you-bad-mistress?bt_email=tammy@tammynelson.org&bt_ts=1462385162690://www.oxfordhandbooks.com/view/10.1093/oxfordhb/9780199376377.001.0001/oxfordhb-9780199376377-e-19#oxfordhb-9780199376377-e-19-div1-8

xxxiii Nelson, Tammy (2012) The New Monogamy; Redefining your relationship After Infidelity, New Harbinger Press, Oakland CA

xxxiv Nelson, Tammy

xxxv Geiss & O'Leary, 1981; Whisman, Dixon, & Johnson, 1997.

xxxvi Peck, M. Scott, The Road Less Traveled

xxxvii Haupert ML, Gesselman AN, Moors AC, Fisher HE, Garcia JR, (2017) Prevalence of Experiences With Consensual Nonmonogamous Relationships:

Made in the USA
Monee, IL
25 November 2024